How to Find
Superior Ingredients
TO ELEVATE
Your Asian
Home Cooking

THE
ASIAN MARKET
COOKBOOK

VIVIAN
ARONSON 袁倩祎

Celebrity chef and founder
of CookingBomb

PAGE STREET
PUBLISHING CO.

PAGE STREET
PUBLISHING CO.

First published in 2021 by
Page Street Publishing Co.
27 Congress Street, Suite 1511
Salem, MA 01970
www.pagestreetpublishing.com

Distributed by Macmillan, sales in Canada by The Canadian Manda Group.

26 25 24 23 22   2 3 4 5 6

ISBN-13: 978-1-64567-448-1
ISBN-10: 1-64567-448-7

Library of Congress Control Number: 2021931948

Cover and book design by Meg Baskis for Page Street Publishing Co.
Photography by Vivian Aronson

Printed and bound in the United States

In memory of my grandma and grandpa, Chen Guo Xuan and Yuan Da Chang, who inspired me and taught me how to cook.

CONTENTS

PRESERVED FOODS 114

SWEETS 136

INTRODUCTION

Growing up during the 1980s and '90s in Chengdu, the capital of Sichuan, China, my family ate virtually all of our meals at home. From when I was a little girl, my parents would send me to the market to buy vegetables, soy sauce and other cooking ingredients. Back then, there were no bottles of brand-name soy sauce or cooking wine, so I would bring empty bottles with me that I would have filled by weight at the store. On the way, I would keep repeating how much of each item I was supposed to buy so that I would not forget.

There were few restaurants in those days and they were considered awfully expensive. In order to eat good food, you needed to know how to cook good food. My grandmother did most of the cooking—she even made her own steamed buns, dumplings, noodles and mochi. A typical home meal in China consists of three to four shared dishes plus rice. Meat was expensive, so most of these dishes were either vegetarian or contained just enough meat to flavor the dish.

Markets in China were different from those in the West. I would buy meat, seafood and vegetables at outdoor markets. While similar to farmers' markets in Western countries, you can also buy live fish, seafood and even chickens at Chinese markets. The vegetables and everything else you buy are weighed on traditional handheld Chinese scales. Most people during that time did not own refrigerators, so you would buy only enough to eat that night and return to the market for the next day's meal. Times have changed! Now there are modern markets selling a myriad of brands and packaged foods just like in the West.

When I shop in Asian markets in the West, shoppers always approach me and ask which brand of an item they should buy. There are so many different bottles of sauces and packages of noodles lining the shelves, so it can be daunting for someone who does not cook Chinese food frequently to navigate the aisles. There may even be a dozen different types of rice to choose from. How can you choose a brand when you cannot even read the Chinese label? I decided to write a book not only to share my love of Chinese food but also to explain how to go about choosing common items in the Asian market. These include common items such as soy sauce and sesame oil, as well as ingredients much less familiar in the West. Have you ever considered buying fermented tofu or Sichuan fermented broad bean chili paste? What about potato noodles or preserved mustard stems? I will tell you what they are and how to cook with them. I will explain the difference between dark and light soy sauces and why they are both added to a dish. After reading this book, I hope that you will be able to successfully navigate any Asian market and be able to create a delicious meal for your family and friends.

CHAPTER 1

SAUCES

Oyster Sauce, *Hao You* 蚝油

Used in many Chinese dishes, high-quality oyster sauce is naturally dark. It is made from oyster extracts, sugar, salt and water. The founder of the **Lee Kum Kee** brand, Lee Kum Sheung, invented this sauce in 1888. This is the brand I use most often. The company also has a vegetarian version made from mushrooms. Refrigerate the bottle after opening it.

Miso Paste 味增

Miso paste is made from fermented soybeans and rice. There are three kinds of miso paste: white miso, red miso and awase miso. The different colors come from the length of time it takes to make the paste. White miso has a lighter flavor, a slightly sweet taste and takes less time to produce than red miso. Red miso has more salt and a richer flavor than white miso. Awase is a combination of white and red miso. Awase is a good choice for all kinds of Japanese cooking. You can buy all different kinds of miso paste and mix them together in your recipe to get a more complex flavor. One of my favorite brands is **Marukome Ryotei No Aji Miso Paste**. This is a high-quality red miso paste blended with *bonito* and *konbu* (kelp) *dashi*. **Miko Awase** miso is another good choice.

Korean *Gochujang* Sauce 韩国辣椒酱

Gochujang is a traditional Korean chili sauce made from glutinous rice, fermented soybeans, red chili pepper flakes and salt. It has a deep red color, a thick consistency like a jam and both sweet and spicy flavors. I love to use it in both meat and vegetable dishes. To pick out an authentic gochujang sauce, find one packed in a red jar with an English label on the back saying "hot pepper paste" or "red pepper paste." Some of the big brands are **Chung Jung Won (Chung Jung One), CJ Haechandle** and **Sempio**. This versatile sauce can be used in noodles, hotpots, vegetables and meat dishes.

Sichuan Broad Bean Chili Paste, *Dou Ban* 豆瓣

Dou ban is called the "soul of Sichuan cuisine." This is the most important ingredient for many Sichuan dishes such as Mapo Tofu (page 20) and Double Cooked Pork Belly (page 16). In Sichuan, we call it *dou ban jiang*, which means "bean paste." It is made with fermented broad—also called fava—beans, *er jingtiao* chili peppers, soybeans and flour. There are many steps involved in making dou ban. First, the chili peppers are chopped and mixed with salt. The broad beans are soaked, boiled, then mixed with ground soybeans and flour and then fermented. After the fermentation process, the broad beans are mixed with the chilis and left to ferment from 6 months to a year. The highest-quality dou ban ferments for a year and a half. The most famous dou ban is made in a small town named Pi Xian and is called *Pi Xian dou ban,* 郫县豆瓣. The most famous brand in Pi Xian is named **Juan Chen** 鹃城. Look for this brand in an Asian market to get the best dou ban jiang, but any dou ban made in Sichuan is quite good. Other well-known brands are **Dan Dan, Chuan Lao Hui** and **Shu Wei Yuan**.

Sweet Wheat Flour Paste, *Tian Mian Jiang* 甜面酱

Tian mian jiang, sweet flour paste made with fermented wheat flour, is different from fermented soybean paste, which is made with soybeans. Sweet wheat flour paste is a thick, smooth, dark brown paste with a savory and sweet flavor. This paste is used in many dishes in Sichuan as well as in northern China. It can be used as a cooking ingredient as well as a dipping sauce. The **Juan Chen** brand also makes Sichuan-style tian mian jiang. Other brands that I use are **ShinHo, Kimlan, Lee Kum Kee** and **Chuan Ba Wang**.

Sesame Paste   Sweet Wheat Flour Paste   Oyster Sauce

Sichuan Broad Bean Chili Paste   Korean Gochujang Sauce   Miso Paste

Sesame Paste, *Zhi Ma Jiang* 芝麻酱

Chinese sesame paste is made from toasted sesame seeds and has a taste that differs from Middle Eastern tahini, which is made from raw sesame seeds. Chinese sesame paste is made from white sesame seeds, whereas Japanese sesame paste is made from roasted black sesame seeds. Many Chinese recipes use white sesame paste, but there are some desserts that use black sesame paste. See the chapter on desserts on how to make Black Sesame Paste (page 154). When you buy sesame paste in an Asian market, it is important to note that some brands add peanuts. I recommend buying brands made from sesame seeds only, so check the ingredients on the package before you buy it. Refrigerate the paste after opening and stir it before refrigerating to help prevent the oil from separating. The brands I like are **Wang Zhi He** 王致和, **Liu Bi Ju** 六必居 and **Lee Kum Kee** 李锦记.

MISO **SALMON**

Wei Zeng San Wen Yu 味增三文鱼

Far and away, Miso Salmon is my kids' favorite fish dish and it is Japanese, not Chinese. It is a great dish to make when you are pressed for time. Use white miso, red miso or awase miso. If you do not have awase, you can use half white and half red miso paste. Mixing two different kinds of miso results in a more complex flavor. White miso is slightly sweet and the red miso is salty and earthy. This gives the fish the sweet-savory flavor that this dish is known for. Just marinate the fish and put it in the broiler for about 10 minutes. Serve it with rice and a salad or a cooked vegetable.

YIELDS 2 SERVINGS

INGREDIENTS

14 oz (400 g) salmon fillets

1 tbsp (15 ml) sake

1 tbsp (15 ml) mirin

1 tbsp (15 ml) soy sauce

2 tbsp (34 g) miso paste

½ tsp sesame oil

1 tsp sesame seeds, for garnish

1 tbsp (6 g) chopped green onion, for garnish

INSTRUCTIONS

Place the salmon fillets in a medium-sized mixing bowl and add the sake, mirin, soy sauce, miso paste and sesame oil. Rub the mixture onto the salmon, cover the bowl with plastic wrap and refrigerate for at least 30 minutes.

When it is ready to cook, set the oven to broil on high and remove the salmon from the marinade, taking care to brush off any excess marinade, which can burn in the broiler. Broil the salmon for 7 to 10 minutes so that it is medium rare and pink inside. Garnish with the sesame seeds and green onion and enjoy!

DOUBLE COOKED PORK BELLY

Hui Guo Rou 回锅肉

YIELDS 4 SERVINGS

INGREDIENTS

2 lb (900 g) pork belly

3½ tsp (7 g) ginger, crushed

1 green onion, cut into 2-inch (5-cm)-long pieces

½ tsp Sichuan peppercorns

2 tbsp (30 ml) cooking oil

3½ tsp (7 g) ginger, sliced

½ tsp salt

2 tbsp (30 g) Sichuan broad bean chili paste (dou ban)

1 tbsp (15 ml) cooking wine

1 tbsp (20 g) fermented black beans

1 tbsp (20 g) sweet wheat flour paste

2 baby leeks or Chinese green garlic, sliced

1 tbsp (15 ml) soy sauce

½ red bell pepper, sliced

During the Qing dynasty, people maintained a shrine to their ancestors in their homes. They would leave various food offerings in the shrine, including boiled pork. At the end of the day, so as not to waste the pork, they would remove it from the shrine and use it to make a dish. Legend has it that someone named Mr. Ling first refried the pork and added the spices to make this now famous dish.

As a child growing up in China, meat was very expensive, so it was a real treat when my grandmother made double cooked pork.

Sichuan broad bean chili paste is my most used sauce since many Sichuan dishes use it. The aroma and taste come out from stir-frying it with cooking oil, so you always want to stir-fry dou ban until the cooking oil is fully infused with the paste and becomes reddish. Then you can add any meat, vegetable or cooked rice to make a fried rice dish with this sauce. The fried rice has a savory, slightly spicy taste. In this classic meat dish, dou ban gives the meat a savory, fragrant, spicy flavor. A slightly sweet taste comes from sweet flour paste and the combination of sauces gives an umami flavor.

INSTRUCTIONS

In a large pot, add the pork belly and fill the pot with water to cover the meat by 2 inches (5 cm). Bring to a boil over high heat and add the crushed ginger, green onion and Sichuan peppercorns. Turn the heat down to low and simmer for another 10 to 15 minutes. Remove the pork from the water and set aside until completely cool. You can do this the day before you want to complete the dish and store the pork in the refrigerator to cook the next day.

When you are ready to finish the dish, slice the pork into thin slices. Then, heat the cooking oil in a wok over high heat and add the pork slices. Stir-fry with the ginger slices and salt until the pork curls up and you see some of the pork fat render. Push the pork to one side of the wok and add the dou ban to the oil and fat in the center of the wok, then stir-fry until the oil is red. Then, mix the sauce with the pork and add the cooking wine. Next, add the black beans and sweet wheat flour paste. Stir-fry until fragrant and then combine with the pork. Lastly, add the leeks, soy sauce and red bell pepper. Stir-fry for another 2 to 3 minutes until cooked and serve.

PHOENIX TAIL IN
SESAME PASTE

Ma Jiang Feng Wei 麻酱凤尾

This dish gets its name from the way the lettuce is laid out on the plate to resemble the tail of the mythical bird *fenghuang*, or phoenix. The sesame paste has a rich nutty flavor but is slightly bitter. Balanced with a little sugar and soy sauce, this crunchy vegetable dish has a rich, toasty flavor. It is essentially a Chinese salad with a sesame dressing and is served as part of a selection of cold dishes eaten as appetizers.

YIELDS 4 SERVINGS

INGREDIENTS

3 tbsp (48 g) sesame paste

1 tbsp (15 ml) sesame oil from the sesame paste jar

1 tbsp (15 ml) soy sauce

1 tsp sugar, plus more to taste

1 tsp chili oil, plus more to taste

3 tbsp (45 ml) cold water or stock

Salt, to taste

¾ lb (340 g) Indian or romaine lettuce

INSTRUCTIONS

Put the sesame paste and the sesame oil in a medium-sized bowl and mix well. Then, add the soy sauce, sugar, chili oil and water. Mix everything together into a smooth sauce. Taste the sauce and add the salt, extra sugar or more chili oil to your liking. Wash, dry and cut the lettuce into 4- to 5-inch (10- to 12-cm)-long pieces. Pour the sauce over the lettuce right before serving.

MAPO
TOFU

Ma Po Dou Fu
麻婆豆腐

INGREDIENTS

1 (14-oz [397-g]) box firm tofu, cut into 1-inch (2.5-cm) cubes

1 quart (946 ml) hot water with ½ tsp salt

3 tbsp (45 ml) canola oil

4 oz (113 g) ground beef

2½ tbsp (38 g) Sichuan broad bean chili paste

1 tbsp (7 g) pickled red pepper, minced, or substitute fresh red pepper, minced

1 tbsp (6 g) fresh ginger, chopped

2 tsp (6 g) dried Sichuan chili powder

1 tsp dried Sichuan peppercorn powder, plus extra for serving

1 tbsp (20 g) fermented black beans

1 cup (236 ml) chicken stock or water

1 tsp sugar

2 tsp (10 ml) soy sauce

Pinch of salt

¼ cup (12 g) Chinese leeks, chopped

4 tsp (10 g) cornstarch mixed with 3 tbsp (45 ml) water

This is one of the most famous and popular Sichuan dishes around the world. There are many different versions, but this is my grandma's recipe—spicy and tongue numbing! This is a perfect dish to eat with rice. For a vegan version, just leave out the beef and use water instead of chicken stock.

INSTRUCTIONS

Put the tofu cubes in a bowl of lightly salted hot water for 1 minute. Then drain out the water, leaving the tofu in the bowl.

Heat the canola oil in a wok over high heat until smoking. Add the ground beef and stir-fry until crispy but not dry. Add the Sichuan broad bean chili paste, minced pickled red pepper and ginger. Turn the heat down to medium and stir-fry the beef with the spices for 30 seconds. Add the Sichuan chili powder, Sichuan peppercorn powder and fermented black beans and stir-fry for another 20 seconds.

Add the chicken stock or water, sugar, soy sauce and a pinch of salt. Mix well and then add the drained tofu. Mix the tofu gently, because otherwise the tofu may crumble. Simmer for 5 minutes or until the tofu has absorbed some of the sauce. Add the leeks and gently combine. Add the cornstarch mixture in three stages, mixing well until the sauce has thickened. Finally, transfer the dish into a serving bowl and garnish with a sprinkling of Sichuan peppercorn powder.

STIR-FRIED
BOK CHOY

Qing Chao Bai Cai
清炒白菜

YIELDS 4 SERVINGS

INGREDIENTS

1 lb (454 g) bok choy, washed and dried

2 tbsp (30 ml) cooking oil

3½ tsp (7 g) ginger, sliced

1 tbsp (15 g) garlic, chopped

10 dried chili peppers (optional)

2 tbsp (30 ml) cooking wine

2 tbsp (30 ml) oyster sauce

½ tsp salt

A green vegetable is always served as part of a Chinese meal. This is a simple preparation that you can use with almost any green vegetable that you find at an Asian market. Oyster sauce tastes like a combination of soy and barbecue sauces. It gives plain vegetables an umami taste. The fresh ginger and garlic add fragrance. For a vegetarian version, use vegetarian oyster sauce or just leave it out altogether.

INSTRUCTIONS

Heat a dry, clean wok over high heat and when the wok is hot, add the bok choy and stir-fry for 2 to 3 minutes, until it has wilted. Remove the bok choy from the wok and set aside.

Add the cooking oil to the hot wok, followed by the ginger, garlic and dried chili peppers, if using. Stir-fry until fragrant. Add the bok choy back into the wok and stir-fry with the spices for about 10 seconds. Add the cooking wine, oyster sauce and salt and then continue to stir-fry for another 30 seconds. Serve immediately while the bok choy still has a slight crisp.

SHREDDED PORK
IN SWEET BEAN SAUCE

Jing Jiang Rou Si
京酱肉丝

YIELDS 2 SERVINGS

INGREDIENTS

MARINADE

1 egg white, beaten

1½ tbsp (23 ml) soy sauce

2 tsp (5 g) cornstarch

½ tbsp (8 ml) cooking wine

PORK

½ lb (227 g) pork tenderloin, sliced into 3-inch (7.5-cm)-long slivers

3 tbsp (45 ml) cooking oil, divided

2 tbsp (40 g) sweet wheat flour paste

1½ tbsp (23 g) ketchup

½ tbsp (8 g) sugar

4 green onions, cut into thin 3-inch (7.5-cm)-long slivers

1 tsp sesame oil

The word *"jing"* in the Chinese name of this dish refers to Beijing, the origin of this stir-fried pork dish with a sweet sauce. The sauce is meant to taste like the one used for Peking duck, and just like Peking duck, it is eaten with green onions and often served with the same pancakes. Both dishes use sweet wheat flour paste, which is both savory and mildly sweet. This paste gives a dark, thick consistency to the meat.

INSTRUCTIONS

In a medium-sized bowl, combine the egg white, soy sauce, cornstarch and cooking wine. Then, add the pork slivers and marinate for 15 minutes.

Heat a wok over high heat and add 2 tablespoons (30 ml) of the cooking oil. When the oil is nearly smoking, add the marinated meat and stir-fry until the meat turns opaque. Remove the pork from the wok and set aside. Heat the remaining 1 tablespoon (15 ml) of the cooking oil and then add the sweet flour paste, ketchup and sugar. Turn the heat down and stir a few times until the sauce is fragrant, about 2 to 3 minutes.

Return the pork to the wok to combine with the sauce and cook for another 30 seconds. Lay the green onion slivers on a serving dish in a decorative pattern of your choice. Serve the pork over the center of the green onions and drizzle the sesame oil on top.

TOFU
WITH FERMENTED BLACK BEANS AND GINGER

Jiang Mo Dou Chi Dou Fu
姜末豆豉豆腐

YIELDS 4 SERVINGS

INGREDIENTS

1 (14-oz [397-g]) box soft tofu

4⅔ tbsp (28 g) chopped ginger

2 tbsp (40 g) fermented black beans

2 tbsp (30 ml) cooking oil

1 tbsp (15 ml) soy sauce

1 tbsp (15 g) sugar

¼ cup (60 ml) warm water

1 tbsp (15 ml) water mixed with 2 tsp (8 g) cornstarch

Pinch of bonito fish flakes, for garnish

I came across this dish about twenty years ago at a restaurant in Chengdu. The restaurant would not give me the recipe, so I recreated it at home. You need the texture of soft tofu for this recipe, because harder tofu is too chewy. The tofu is steamed and the sauce is poured over, so you can eat this with a spoon. The bonito flakes are my own addition since they are not a Chinese ingredient.

INSTRUCTIONS

Steam the tofu over high heat for 10 minutes or you can leave it out until it reaches room temperature. Chop the ginger and fermented black beans and set aside.

Heat your wok over high heat and add the cooking oil. Then, turn the burner down to medium-high and add the ginger and fermented black beans. Stir-fry until fragrant, about 1 to 2 minutes.

Add the soy sauce and sugar, followed by the warm water. Cook for about 2 minutes. Add the cornstarch mixture and stir until the sauce thickens, about 30 seconds. Place the tofu on a serving dish and pour the sauce over the tofu. Garnish with bonito fish flakes and serve.

MISO
SOUP

Wei Zeng Tang 味增汤

YIELDS 4 SERVINGS

INGREDIENTS

DASHI

½ tsp dried *wakame* (dried seaweed) and ½ cup (120 ml) warm water, to soak

½ cup (21 g) dried seaweed kelp

1 quart (946 ml) water

1¾ cups (21 g) bonito flakes

3 tbsp (54 g) miso paste

⅓ cup (80 ml) warm water

1 (14-oz [397-g]) box silken tofu

1 tbsp (6 g) chopped green onion, for garnish

This is my kids' favorite soup. They eat it as a meal with rice added into the bowl. I make at least 4 liters of dashi, the soup base, at a time and freeze it in 1-liter containers. I defrost it overnight in the refrigerator and just bring it to a boil for dinner the next evening. Then I add the miso paste, wakame and tofu and serve.

INSTRUCTIONS

In a small bowl, soak the dried wakame in water and set aside. Rinse the dried seaweed kelp with cold water, place in a pot, add 1 quart (946 ml) of water and boil for 30 minutes. Turn off the heat, add the bonito flakes and let soak in the seaweed soup for 15 to 20 minutes with the lid on. Remove the seaweed and strain the soup through a sieve to remove the flakes. You now have dashi.

Put the dashi back in the pot, bring to a simmer over high heat and then turn off the heat. In a medium-sized bowl, mix the miso paste with ⅓ cup (80 ml) of warm water and add the mixture to the dashi, and then stir until combined. Cut the tofu into cubes and add them to the soup, then drain and add the wakame. Serve in individual soup bowls and garnish with green onion.

HOMEMADE
KIMCHI

Han Guo Pao Cai
韩国泡菜

YIELDS ABOUT 1
(1-QUART [1-L]) JAR

INGREDIENTS

½ cup (146 g) sea salt

1¼ cups (300 ml) water, divided

5 lb (2.3 kg) Napa cabbage leaves, separated and washed

1 bulb garlic

½ onion, chopped

½ cup (67 g) Korean chili powder

6 green onions, chopped

1 tbsp (15 g) Korean hot pepper paste (gochujang)

This is my version of Korean kimchi. I don't add fish sauce or dried shrimp to my kimchi, but you can add them if you like. In this recipe, I added gochujang sauce, my favorite Korean sauce. The spicy and salty flavor is perfect for Napa cabbage. Kimchi is made differently from Chinese pickles (page 134). To make my kimchi, the cabbage is wet brined, then placed in a jar with spices to ferment for several days. I tried using Sichuan red pepper powder for kimchi instead of Korean red pepper, but the Sichuan red pepper was too spicy, even for me.

INSTRUCTIONS

In a large bowl, combine the sea salt and 1 cup (240 ml) of water. Add the washed Napa cabbage leaves and let them soak in the brine for 2 hours. Boil a large clean glass jar to sterilize it, remove it from the pot and let it dry completely. Peel the garlic cloves and put them in a blender with the chopped onion and ¼ cup (60 ml) of water. Blend the mixture into a paste. Put the garlic paste in a bowl and add the chili powder, chopped green onions and gochujang.

Rinse and dry the cabbage, and then place it back in the bowl and add the sauce. Mix well. Pack the seasoned cabbage into the sterilized jar and close the lid. Store at room temperature for 5 to 7 days until fermented. Use clean chopsticks to remove a portion of the kimchi from the jar. Keep refrigerated after opening.

TYPHOON SHELTER

TEA-FLAVORED SHRIMP

Bi Feng Tang Cha Xiang Xia 避风塘茶香虾

YIELDS 2 SERVINGS

INGREDIENTS

½ lb (227 g) medium shrimp

½ red bell pepper

3½ tbsp (21 g) green tea leaves (use any green tea, but I prefer to use oolong tea)

2 cups (480 ml) hot water, for brewing tea

1 tbsp (15 ml) cooking wine

4 tbsp (60 ml) cooking oil, divided

1–2 tbsp (6–12 g) chopped green onions

1 tbsp (15 ml) soy sauce

2 cups (112 g) panko bread crumbs

1 tsp salt

This is a Hong Kong (China) dish that gets its name from the small bays around Hong Kong island used as boat shelters during typhoons. Many people lived permanently on boats in these shelters and developed their own food and culture. In China, the shrimp would be cooked and served in the shell, sometimes with the head on as well. At home I use shelled and deveined shrimp because it absorbs the sauce better and is much less messy to eat. When I cook shrimp in the shell at home, I spend most of my meal peeling the shrimp for my kids. The crispy tea leaves add a crunchy texture to the dish.

INSTRUCTIONS

Shell, clean and devein the shrimp, unless you have bought cleaned shrimp. Cut the red bell pepper into ¼-inch (6-mm) slices. Using a large teacup or small bowl, soak the green tea leaves in 2 cups (480 ml) of hot water, cover and let brew for 15 minutes. Drain the tea, reserving the liquid tea in a bowl for the marinade and the tea leaves for stir-frying. Dry the tea leaves with a paper towel and set aside. Let the bowl of liquid tea cool to room temperature, add the shrimp and cooking wine to the bowl and marinate for 15 minutes. Then, remove the shrimp from the marinade, dry the shrimp with a paper towel and discard the marinade liquid.

In a wok, heat 2 tablespoons (30 ml) of cooking oil over medium-high heat. When the oil reaches about 180°F (80°C), add the tea leaves, turn the heat to low and stir-fry the leaves until crispy. If the oil temperature is too high, the tea leaves will burn. When crispy, remove the tea leaves from the oil and drain on a paper towel. Heat 2 tablespoons (30 ml) of cooking oil in the wok over high heat, add the green onions and stir-fry for about 20 seconds. Add the shrimp and stir-fry for about 30 seconds until the shrimp turn opaque and then add the soy sauce. Add the panko bread crumbs and salt, turn the heat to low and stir-fry until the panko bread crumbs turn golden brown. Turn off the heat and add the crispy tea leaves and red bell pepper slices, mixing well. Serve immediately while still hot for the best flavor.

SICHUAN-STYLE
SPICY FISH

Fei Teng Yu 沸腾鱼

YIELDS 4 SERVINGS

INGREDIENTS

1 lb (454 g) tilapia fillets cut into ¼-inch (6-mm)-thick slices

¼ tsp salt

3 tbsp (45 ml) Chinese cooking wine

1 tsp cornstarch

½ lb (227 g) fresh bean sprouts or any green vegetable of your choice (celery, broccoli, cucumbers)

6 tbsp (90 ml) canola oil, divided

3 tbsp (45 g) Sichuan broad bean chili paste

2½ tsp (5 g) Sichuan peppercorns, divided

18–24 dried red chili peppers, divided

5 cloves garlic, sliced

7½ tsp (15 g) peeled and thinly sliced ginger

4 green onions, chopped, divided

3 cups (720 ml) chicken stock or hot water

1 tbsp (15 ml) soy sauce

½ tsp sugar

This is an extremely popular way to prepare fish in Sichuan and I cook it at home all the time. In China, people buy whole freshwater fish at the market and filet them at home. After the dish is prepared, hot, fragrant chili and Sichuan peppercorn oil is poured over the top. The hot oil continues cooking the fish. The combination of dou ban, chili oil and Sichuan chili oil add not just heat but a complex flavor to the fish. Make sure you have enough rice to eat with the dish so that you can eat it mixed with the soup.

INSTRUCTIONS

Add the fish slices to the marinade mixture of the salt, Chinese cooking wine and cornstarch and set aside. Blanch the vegetables for 30 seconds in boiling water and then drain and lay them on the bottom of a deep serving bowl. It must be able to hold the fish, vegetables and soup.

Heat 2 tablespoons (30 ml) of the oil in a wok over high heat until smoking, and then add the Sichuan chili paste and stir-fry until the oil turns red, about 30 seconds. Add ½ teaspoon Sichuan peppercorns and 6 to 12 dried chili peppers, stir-frying constantly for 30 seconds to avoid burning the spices. After 30 seconds, add the garlic, ginger and 2 chopped green onions and stir-fry for about 30 more seconds. Add the chicken stock or hot water and bring to a boil. Stir in the soy sauce and sugar. Gently place the fish slices into the wok. Cook over medium heat until the fish turns opaque, about 3 minutes. Do not overcook the fish.

When cooked, pour the fish and the soup into the prepared serving bowl with the vegetables on the bottom. To make the chili oil, heat the remaining 4 tablespoons (60 ml) oil in a wok over high heat, add the remaining 12 chili peppers and 2 teaspoons (4 g) Sichuan peppercorns and stir-fry for about 15 seconds. Do not let the spices burn. Pour the oil with the spices directly over the fish in the serving bowl. The oil will continue to cook the fish. Garnish with 2 chopped green onions and serve right away!

CHAPTER 2

CONDIMENTS

Soy Sauce, *Jiang You* 酱油

Chinese soy sauce is brewed with soybeans, wheat, salt, yeast and water and sometimes sugar is added. Naturally brewed soy sauce usually takes 6 months to ferment, but some are aged for a couple of years. It is best to use brewed aged soy sauce and to avoid soy sauce produced with preservatives and diluted with water. For example, try to avoid soy sauce that is only 50% brewed soy sauce with added water and other chemicals. Check the ingredients listed on the label to ensure the soy sauce is brewed with the most basic ingredients. I only use premium aged soy sauce for my dishes. Light soy sauce is called *sheng chou* 生抽, is thinner and lighter in color and has more intense umami flavor. It is good for everyday use. Dark soy sauce, *lao chou* 老抽, is aged longer than light soy sauce, so the color is much darker and contains molasses or another sweetener. I only use dark soy sauce for dishes such as braised meat to add a dark color to the dish. My trick to test for a good bottle of soy sauce is to shake the bottle. Good soy sauce forms little bubbles after shaking and bubbles in better soy sauces last longer. Good soy sauce also lingers longer on the sides of the bottle than chemically produced ones. The brands I like to use are **Wan Ja Shan, Lee Kum Kee** and **ShinHo**.

Chinese Cooking Wine, *Liao Jiu* 料酒

Chinese cooking wine is a key ingredient in many Chinese dishes. The ingredients are rice, wheat and water. Chinese cooking wine is called *liao jiu* 料酒, but labels will say *"huangjiu,"* meaning yellow wine, because liao jiu is a type of huangjiu used in cooking. The most popular one in the United States is Shaoxing wine, which is named after a major wine-producing town in China. Cooking wine has a lower percentage of alcohol compared to drinking wine, huangjiu. When you pick cooking wine, look for an alcohol content of 10 to 15% and a dark orange color. In China, cooking wine is used to marinate meat and fish to improve their aroma and tenderize during the cooking process, which evaporates the alcohol. The brands I like to use are **Asian Taste (Dong Zhi Wei), Ta Pai** and **Wang Zhi He**, which are naturally brewed and fermented.

Chinese Vinegar, *Xiang Cu* 香醋

Chinese vinegar is an inky black vinegar. It is made with water, glutinous rice, wheat bran, sugar and salt. Good-quality vinegar is dark in color with an acidity of more than 5.5 grams per 100 milliliters. Look for this ratio on the label when you are choosing which vinegar to use. The most popular vinegar is Zhenjiang vinegar (Zhenjiang is a city in China). It is mildly acidic—less than distilled white vinegar—with a faintly sweet flavor. I use vinegar in many braised meat and fish dishes, cold appetizers and dumpling dipping sauce. It is also used with chopped ginger as a classic dipping sauce for steamed seafood such as shrimp, crab and lobster. The brands I use are **Hengsun Zheng Jiang** and **Gold Plum Chinkiang Vinegar**.

Sesame Oil, *Xiang You* 香油

In China, we call sesame oil *xiang you* 香油. *"Xiang"* means "fragrant" and *"you"* means "oil." Good-quality sesame oil has a deep sesame fragrance. There are two types of sesame oils: roasted sesame oil and light sesame oil. Roasted sesame oil is the sesame oil extracted from roasted sesame seeds which are cold-pressed to create the finished product. Light sesame oil is extracted from sesame seeds by pressing but does not undergo roasting. Therefore, it is usually pale in color and has a mild flavor. For most of my dishes, I use roasted sesame oil. The classic Sichuan hotpot dipping sauce is mainly sesame oil with chopped garlic. The brands I use are **Kadoya** and **Lee Kum Kee**.

Sesame Oil

Chinese Cooking Wine

Chinese Vinegar

Aged Soy Sauce

SUPERIOR STOCK

Gao Tang 高汤

YIELDS ABOUT
3 QUARTS (3 L)

INGREDIENTS

2 lb (900 g) pork leg bones, or use neck bones or ribs

2 lb (900 g) chicken legs or chicken bones

4 quarts (3.8 L) water

4 green onions

5 tbsp (30 g) ginger, crushed

This is a chicken and pork stock used to flavor many different kinds of dishes. It often contains a piece of Chinese ham, but you may add any ham you have on hand. You can also use chicken bones instead of chicken legs. Because many of the recipes call for a small amount of stock, freeze some in an ice cube tray and when frozen, transfer the cubes to a plastic freezer bag.

INSTRUCTIONS

Put the pork bones and chicken legs in a pot of cold water and bring to a boil for about 2 minutes. Transfer the ingredients to a colander and rinse under cold water. Place the blanched pork bones and chicken legs in the stock pot, add 4 quarts (3.8 L) of cold water and bring to a boil, skimming any foam that rises to the top. Tie the green onions into knots (so they fit in the pot better) and add them to the pot along with the ginger. Cover with a partially closed lid and simmer for 3 to 4 hours.

At the end of the cooking process, the broth should be reduced by at least one-fourth of the original volume. Strain the stock and store it in containers. The stock will keep for a few days in the refrigerator or for a few months in the freezer.

SESAME
CHICKEN

Zhi Ma Ji 芝麻鸡

YIELDS 4 SERVINGS

INGREDIENTS

CHICKEN MARINADE

1 lb (454 g) boneless chicken thighs, cut into 1-inch (2.5-cm) cubes

1 egg white, beaten

2 tbsp (16 g) cornstarch

½ tsp salt

½ tsp sugar

¼ tsp white pepper

SAUCE

½ cup (120 ml) soy sauce

¼ cup (60 ml) gao tang (page 40) or water

½ tsp sesame oil

3 tbsp (45 ml) honey

2 tbsp (30 ml) rice vinegar

2 tsp (4 g) chopped ginger

2 tsp (10 g) minced garlic

1 tbsp (8 g) cornstarch

2 tsp (6 g) sesame seeds

2 tbsp (30 ml) cooking oil

1 green onion, minced, for garnish

1 tsp sesame seeds, for garnish

This is a traditional Chinese version of a popular Chinese American dish that is deep fried and served with a very sweet sauce. In this version, the chicken is stir-fried and the sauce is not nearly as sweet. In China we would use a cut-up chicken on the bone, but this recipe uses boneless chicken thighs. You could substitute chicken breast if you prefer. The sesame oil gives a rich nutty taste and toasted sesame aroma. The toasted sesame seeds add a crunchy texture to the chicken.

INSTRUCTIONS

Place the chicken in a small bowl. Add the egg white, cornstarch, salt, sugar and white pepper. Mix well and let it marinate for 15 minutes. In another small bowl, stir together the soy sauce, gao tang, sesame oil, honey, rice vinegar, ginger, minced garlic, cornstarch and sesame seeds. Set the sauce aside.

Add the cooking oil to a wok and heat it over high heat. Wait until the wok is very hot, then swirl the skillet to make sure the oil coats the entire surface. Add the marinated chicken and stir-fry until golden brown, about 4 minutes. When adding the sauce to the chicken, stir and coat the chicken evenly, gently stirring the chicken in the sauce until it thickens, about 30 seconds. Then, turn off the heat and serve the chicken garnished with green onion and sesame seeds.

SWEET AND SOUR PORK RIBS

Tang Cu Pai Gu 糖醋排骨

This is one of my kids' favorite dishes. Pro tip: Ask the butcher to cut the ribs for you—otherwise, you will need a meat cleaver to cut them yourself. Alternatively, look for precut ribs in an Asian market at the meat counter. In this recipe, the sweetness from the sugar is balanced by the vinegar. Chinese vinegar tastes less acidic than Western vinegar and has a slightly sweet taste as well. My kids love to eat rice with some of the leftover sauce drizzled on top.

INGREDIENTS

2 lb (900 g) baby back ribs, cut into 1½-inch (4-cm)-long pieces

2 green onions, 1 chopped into 2-inch (5-cm)-long pieces, 1 finely chopped for garnish

1-inch (2.5-cm) peeled ginger, sliced into thin rounds

2 whole star anise

2 tbsp (30 ml) Chinese cooking wine

4 tbsp (60 ml) cooking oil

3 tbsp (45 g) sugar

⅓ cup (80 ml) liquid left over from cooking the ribs

3 tbsp (45 ml) aged or regular Chinese soy sauce

½ tsp salt

3 tbsp (45 ml) Chinese vinegar

1 tsp white sesame seeds, for garnish

INSTRUCTIONS

Place the rib pieces in a pot and add enough water to cover the ribs by 2 inches (5 cm). Add the chopped green onion pieces, ginger, star anise and cooking wine. Bring the water to a boil, skim the foam and then simmer the water over low heat for 40 minutes. Using a colander, drain the water, reserving ⅓ cup (80 ml) of the liquid for later.

Using a wok, heat the cooking oil over high heat until smoking, add the ribs and stir-fry them until golden brown, about 5 minutes. Drain the oil and set the ribs aside, leaving about 2 tablespoons (30 ml) of oil in the wok. Add the sugar to the wok with the oil and cook over medium heat, stirring constantly with a spatula to dissolve the sugar. The syrup will boil quickly at first, but as it thickens it will appear to slow down. The edges of the syrup will darken first. When you see the color changing, stir the syrup so it caramelizes evenly and does not burn.

When the sugar has caramelized to a dark brown color after about 3 minutes, return the ribs to the wok, stirring constantly to coat them well with the caramelized sugar. Add the reserved ⅓ cup (80 ml) of liquid, soy sauce, salt and vinegar. Cook the ribs for about 1 minute or until the sauce has thickened. Transfer the ribs and sauce to a serving dish and garnish with chopped green onion and sesame seeds.

LION'S HEAD
MEATBALLS

Shi Zi Tou 狮子头

YIELDS 4 SERVINGS

INGREDIENTS

1 lb (454 g) ground pork

2 tbsp (30 ml) light soy sauce, divided

2 tsp (12 g) salt, divided

1 tbsp (15 ml) cooking wine

2 tsp (4 g) chopped ginger

2 tsp (5 g) cornstarch

1 egg, beaten

8 pieces water chestnuts, finely chopped

3 tbsp (45 ml) cooking oil

2 green onions, 1 chopped into 2-inch (5-cm) pieces, 1 finely chopped for garnish

2 whole star anise

1 tbsp (15 ml) dark soy sauce

4 tsp (20 g) sugar

1 cup (240 ml) water used for boiling the meatballs

This braised pork meatball dish is actually a Shanghai dish and my mother's signature dish. She worked for a company whose workers were mostly originally from Shanghai and her coworkers taught her how to make this dish. The extra sauce is delicious over rice. Since this dish is not spicy, it is perfect for kids. You can serve the meatballs on top of a stir-fried green vegetable or mashed potatoes which also get flavored with the sauce. In this dish as well as many throughout this book, I use soy sauce and cooking wine. Soy sauce is essential not just in Chinese cooking, but in all Asian cuisine. Soy sauce gives both color and deep flavor to dishes. Chinese cooking wine is used in many meat and seafood dishes because it removes the fishy smell from seafood and the greasiness from meat. It adds depth and flavor complexity to every dish.

INSTRUCTIONS

Put the ground pork in a medium-sized mixing bowl, add 1 tablespoon (15 ml) of the light soy sauce, 1 teaspoon of salt, the cooking wine, chopped ginger, cornstarch and the beaten egg. Add the chopped water chestnuts and mix well, stirring in one direction. Bring 3 quarts (3 L) of water to a boil, then turn the heat to low and let it simmer while you prepare the meatballs.

Make the meatballs by taking a portion of the meat mixture into your hands and rolling it between your palms. One pound (454 g) of meat can make eight big meatballs or adjust the size to make smaller ones. Increase the heat under the pot of water to high and gently add the meatballs one by one with a slotted spoon. Boil the meatballs for 6 minutes, then remove them from the water with a slotted spoon and place them in a colander to drain. Reserve a cup (240 ml) of the water for the sauce.

Heat the cooking oil in a wok over high heat until smoking and add the drained meatballs carefully one by one to the oil. Brown the meatballs in the oil, turning them every 30 seconds until evenly browned, for 2 to 3 minutes. Add the 2-inch (5-cm) pieces of green onions and star anise and stir-fry for about 1 minute or until the meatballs are fragrant. Add the remaining 1 tablespoon (15 ml) of light soy sauce, the dark soy sauce, remaining 1 teaspoon of salt, sugar and the reserved cup (240 ml) of cooking liquid. Cook the meatballs in the sauce over medium heat for 6 to 8 minutes until the sauce has thickened. Serve with the chopped green onion as a garnish.

RED-
BRAISED
EGGPLANT

Hong Shao Qie Zi

红烧茄子

YIELDS 4 SERVINGS

INGREDIENTS

2 long Asian eggplants, about 1 lb (454 g)

1 tsp salt

4 tbsp (60 ml) canola oil, divided

1 green onion, chopped

1 tbsp (15 g) sliced garlic

7 tsp (14 g) chopped ginger

2 star anise

2 tbsp (30 ml) cooking wine

1 tsp sugar

2 tbsp (30 ml) soy sauce

½ cup (120 ml) gao tang (page 40) or water

1 tsp cornstarch mixed with 2 tbsp (30 ml) water

1 tbsp (1 g) chopped cilantro, for garnish

Less well-known than Fish Fragrant Eggplant, *Yu Xiang Qie Zi*, red-braised refers to the color of the soy-based sauce in the dish. Soy sauce not only adds depth of flavor but gives a reddish-brown color to the dish. The star anise lends a mild licorice flavor. It is a popular way to serve eggplant in Sichuan, China. You could eat this dish with rice for a simple lunch. Use water instead of chicken stock for a vegan version.

INSTRUCTIONS

Cylindrical vegetables are often cut up using a technique called roll-cutting. Roll-cut pieces have a larger surface area, which allows them to cook faster. Roll-cut the eggplants into 3-inch (7.5-cm)-long pieces by first holding your knife at a 45-degree angle and cutting off a 3-inch (7.5-cm) piece from one end of the eggplant. Then, roll the eggplant one-third of the way around and cut off another 3-inch (7.5-cm) piece at a 45-degree angle. Continue to roll and cut until the eggplant has been completely cut up. Sprinkle the pieces with the salt. Marinate the eggplant for 15 minutes, then squeeze out the black juice.

Heat a wok over high heat, add 2 tablespoons (30 ml) of the canola oil and stir-fry the eggplant until golden brown, 3 to 4 minutes. Remove the eggplant to a dish lined with paper towels to absorb the excess oil. Heat the remaining cooking oil in the wok over high heat and add the green onion, garlic, ginger and star anise. Stir-fry for about 30 seconds until the spices are fragrant, then return the eggplant to the wok and stir-fry with the spices until the eggplant is soft, for about 1 minute. Add the cooking wine, sugar, soy sauce and gao tang and cook over high heat until the liquid boils. Add the cornstarch mixture and continue to cook for about 30 seconds or until the sauce thickens. Transfer to a serving bowl and garnish with chopped cilantro.

COKE CHICKEN LEGS

Ke Le Ji Tui 可乐鸡腿

YIELDS 4 SERVINGS

INGREDIENTS

2 lb (900 g) chicken drumsticks, about 5 legs

4 tsp (8 g) peeled ginger, chopped fine

5 tbsp (75 ml) cooking wine, divided

½ tsp salt

3 tbsp (45 ml) cooking oil

4 tsp (8 g) peeled ginger, sliced thin

1 tbsp (15 g) peeled garlic, sliced

3 whole star anise

1 tsp Sichuan peppercorns

3 tbsp (45 ml) light soy sauce

1 tbsp (15 ml) dark soy sauce

1 cup (240 ml) gao tang (page 40) or water

1 (12-oz [355-ml]) bottle Coca-Cola ®

This dish does not taste as sweet as it sounds because the cola is diluted in water and the sugar is balanced with soy sauce, salt and spices. You can substitute the legs with any part of the chicken you wish and of course you can use any brand of cola. When the sauce thickens, it creates a nice glaze over the chicken. Traditionally, this chicken dish uses rock sugar, but the cola brings a stronger flavor with caramel notes to this soy-based sauce.

INSTRUCTIONS

In a medium bowl marinate the chicken legs with the chopped ginger, 3 tablespoons (45 ml) of cooking wine and salt for 20 minutes.

Heat the oil in a wok over high heat and stir-fry the marinated chicken for about 4 minutes or until golden brown. Add the ginger slices, garlic, star anise and Sichuan peppercorns and stir-fry with the chicken legs for about 30 seconds. Then, add the remaining cooking wine and both soy sauces. Add the gao tang and cook until the liquid is boiling, then add the bottle of Coca-Cola. Cook over low heat for 25 minutes or until the sauce thickens. Serve hot.

LAMB
WITH
SCALLIONS

Cong Bao Yang Rou
葱爆羊肉

YIELDS 4 SERVINGS

INGREDIENTS

¾ lb (340 g) thinly sliced lamb loin

3 tbsp (45 ml) canola oil

4 green onions, thinly sliced

2 tbsp (30 ml) soy sauce

1 tbsp (15 ml) cooking wine

¼ tsp salt

1 tsp sesame oil

This is a northern Chinese dish. The dish uses a small amount of very thinly sliced lamb, which is cooked very quickly in a very hot wok with oil. If you use too much meat or if the oil is not hot enough, the lamb will not sear properly and the juices will run out. The combination of onion, soy, wine and sesame enhances the natural flavor of the lamb. If you want to double or triple the recipe, consider making it in 10.7-ounce (300-g) batches.

INSTRUCTIONS

If you buy frozen lamb slices, defrost them first and dry the meat with a paper towel. Heat a wok over high heat and add the canola oil.

When the oil is hot, add the dried-off lamb slices and stir-fry for 20 seconds or until seared. Add the green onions and quickly stir-fry with the lamb for 30 seconds. Add the soy sauce, cooking wine and salt and continue to stir-fry until well combined. Place the lamb and scallions on a serving platter and drizzle the sesame oil over the dish before serving.

HOMESTYLE
TOFU

Jia Chang Dou Fu
家常豆腐

YIELDS 4 SERVINGS

INGREDIENTS

1 (14-oz [397-g]) box firm tofu

10 tbsp (56 g) Chinese garlic scapes or baby leeks, chopped

3 tbsp (45 ml) cooking oil

Pinch of salt, plus more to taste

¼ lb (113 g) sliced pork belly, or bacon if pork belly is not available

3⅔ tbsp (55 g) Sichuan broad bean chili paste

3 tbsp (45 ml) soy sauce

1 tbsp (15 ml) cooking wine

½ cup (120 ml) hot water

2 tsp (5 g) cornstarch mixed with 3 tbsp (45 ml) water

As the name suggests, this is an everyday cook-at-home tofu dish in Sichuan, China. It is spicy due to the Sichuan broad bean chili paste, which is stir-fried in oil to release the chili oil. You can adjust the amount of chili paste to your liking or just leave it out.

In China, the tofu is blanched in salt water before use as this dries it out so that it gets crispier when stir-fried. Feel free to skip this step.

INSTRUCTIONS

Cut the tofu into 1 x 1½–inch (2.5 x 4–cm) pieces. Boil salted water and blanch the tofu for 2 to 3 minutes, then dry well. Chop the Chinese garlic scapes into 2-inch (5-cm) pieces.

Heat the cooking oil over medium heat, sprinkle a pinch of salt into the wok, then carefully place the tofu in the oil. Stir-fry both sides for about 3 minutes or until golden brown, then remove the tofu and place on a dish with a paper towel underneath the tofu.

Heat the remaining oil in the wok over high heat, add the pork and stir-fry until cooked through, about 2 minutes. Push the pork to one side of the wok and add the Sichuan broad bean chili paste to the oil. Fry for a few seconds until the oil is red, then mix together with the pork. Add the soy sauce, cooking wine and hot water, stir-fry a few times and then add the cooked tofu back into the wok. Turn the heat to low and cook the tofu and pork in the sauce for 2 minutes. Add the garlic scapes and cook for another minute. Turn the heat to high and add salt to taste followed by the cornstarch mixture. Carefully mix well for about 30 seconds or until the sauce thickens.

FISH FRAGRANT SHREDDED PORK

Yu Xiang Rou Si 鱼香肉丝

YIELDS 4 SERVINGS

INGREDIENTS

5–6 dried wood ear mushrooms

½ lb (227 g) pork tenderloin

⅜ tsp salt, divided

1 tsp cornstarch

1 tbsp (15 ml) Chinese cooking wine

¼ cup (60 ml) gao tang (page 40) or water

1 tbsp (15 ml) soy sauce

1 tbsp (15 ml) Chinese vinegar

1 tbsp (15 g) sugar

1 tsp potato starch or cornstarch mixed with 3 tbsp (45 ml) water

5 tbsp (75 ml) cooking oil

3 tsp (15 g) minced ginger

2 tbsp (30 g) minced garlic

1 tbsp (7 g) chopped pickled red chili peppers

10 tbsp (56 g) pea shoots

5 tbsp (30 g) chopped green onion

1 tbsp (15 ml) red chili oil (optional)

This famous Sichuan dish uses the same sauce as Fish Fragrant Eggplant, **Yu Xiang Qie Zi** 鱼香茄子. As the story goes, this sauce was originally used to cook fish. A Sichuan housewife had leftover sauce that she did not want to waste, so she used it to cook pork and served it to her husband, who loved it. This dish has a complex but delicious taste that is salty, sweet, sour, spicy and fresh, not fishy at all!

INSTRUCTIONS

In a medium-sized bowl, soak the wood ear mushrooms in hot water for 30 minutes, then drain. Cut the pork into slivers, about ⅛ inch (3 mm) thick and 3 inches (7.5 cm) long. Place the pork in a medium-sized bowl with ¼ teaspoon of salt, the cornstarch and Chinese cooking wine. Mix well and marinate for 15 minutes.

Make the sauce by combining the gao tang, ⅛ teaspoon of salt, soy sauce, vinegar, sugar and starch-water slurry in a small bowl. Heat a wok over high heat and add the cooking oil. When the oil is hot, add the marinated pork and quickly stir-fry, separating the pork slivers, for about 2 minutes or until the pork is opaque. Add the ginger, garlic and pickled peppers. Continue to stir-fry until the oil is red, about 1 minute. Add the wood ear mushrooms and pea shoots, stir-frying everything together until combined.

Pour in the sauce mixture, mixing well to incorporate it. Then, add the green onion and continue to mix well and cook for 1 minute. Place the finished pork on a serving platter and drizzle some red chili oil on top, if desired, for an extra kick.

CHICKEN
WITH
SHIITAKE
MUSH-
ROOMS

Xiang Gu Men Ji
香茹焖鸡

YIELDS 4 SERVINGS

INGREDIENTS

1½ cups + 4 tsp (57 g) dried shiitake mushrooms

3 tbsp (45 ml) canola oil, divided

1 tbsp (15 g) rock sugar

1½ lb (680 g) chicken on the bone and with the skin on, chopped into 3-inch (7.5-cm) pieces

3⅓ tbsp (20 g) ginger, peeled and thinly sliced

2 green onions, cut into 1-inch (2.5-cm)-long pieces

½ tsp Sichuan peppercorns

3 star anise

2 bay leaves

1 cinnamon stick

2 tbsp (30 ml) light soy sauce

1 tsp dark soy sauce

2 tbsp (30 ml) cooking wine

½ tsp salt

1⅔ cups (400 ml) hot water

Steamed rice, for serving

This is a red-braised dish often eaten in the winter. The dried shiitake mushrooms give the chicken a meaty, smoky flavor which you do not get from fresh mushrooms. The chicken and mushrooms are believed to have healing properties. The flavor of this dish will improve overnight, but you can eat it right away.

INSTRUCTIONS

In a medium-sized bowl, soak the shiitake mushrooms in hot water for 1 hour until softened. Cut the larger ones in half. Heat 2 tablespoons (30 ml) of the canola oil in a wok over high heat and when hot, add the rock sugar. When the sugar has melted, add the chicken and stir-fry until the chicken has caramelized, about 5 minutes. It should have a golden color. Remove from the wok and set aside.

Heat 1 tablespoon (15 ml) of canola oil in the wok over high heat and add the ginger, green onions, Sichuan peppercorns, star anise, bay leaves and cinnamon stick. Stir-fry for about 30 seconds or until fragrant. Return the chicken to the wok and stir-fry with the spices for 20 seconds, then add the light and dark soy sauces, cooking wine and salt. Add the hot water and bring to a boil. Turn the heat to low and cook for 25 minutes. Add the shiitake mushrooms and simmer for another 20 minutes. Discard the bay leaves and serve hot with steamed rice.

STEAMED
EGG
CUSTARD

Zheng Da Geng 蒸蛋羹

YIELDS 2 SERVINGS

INGREDIENTS

3 large eggs, beaten

¾ cup (180 ml) warm water

⅛ tsp salt

1 tbsp (15 ml) soy sauce, for garnish

1 tbsp (6 g) chopped green onion, for garnish

This is a dish that parents often make for their kids to eat for any meal. I usually serve it to my kids for dinner. It is a light nondairy custard and it can be served with a ground pork or chicken topping. A vegetarian option would be to serve it topped with a stir-fried mushroom and green onion topping. You can use the meat topping from the Dan Dan Noodles recipe (page 75).

INSTRUCTIONS

Beat the eggs first and then add the warm water and salt. Mix well. Strain the mixture through a sieve into a heatproof glass or ceramic bowl to create a smoother texture. Cover the bowl with plastic wrap.

Boil water in the bottom of a steamer and once boiling, place the bowl inside. Steam for 15 minutes until the custard is firm. Serve garnished with the soy sauce and green onion. To make the dish gluten free, use coconut aminos or a gluten-free soy sauce.

STEAMED WHOLE FISH

Qing Zheng Quan Yu
清蒸全鱼

YIELDS 4 SERVINGS

INGREDIENTS

1 whole sea bass, about 1½ lb (680 g), cleaned and scaled

2 tsp (12 g) salt

3 tbsp (45 ml) cooking wine

5–6 pieces thinly sliced ginger

2 green onions, 1 cut into 2-inch (5-cm) pieces, 1 minced for garnish, divided

¼ cup (60 ml) hot gao tang (page 40)

3 tbsp (45 ml) soy sauce

2 tbsp (30 ml) hot canola oil

In China, people will buy a live fish at the market and have it cleaned and scaled. There are some Asian markets in the United States that sell live fish, but if you cannot find one, just make sure you ask the fishmonger to clean and scale the fish for you. This dish can be made with a variety of fish such as snapper, tilapia or grouper. If you prefer fish fillets, you could substitute halibut, tilapia or sea bass fillets. A sauce consisting of stock, soy sauce and oil poured over the cooked fish gives a rich and slightly salty flavor to the dish.

INSTRUCTIONS

Score the fish diagonally on both sides. In a large bowl, marinate the fish with the salt and cooking wine for 10 to 15 minutes. Place the fish on a heatproof plate and place the ginger slices and cut green onion pieces in the diagonal cuts on top of the fish and in the cut on the fish belly.

Boil water in the bottom of a steamer and once the water boils, place the plate with the fish inside. Steam covered for 10 minutes. To serve, place the fish on a long serving dish that can hold some liquid. Pour the gao tang, soy sauce and hot oil over the fish and garnish with the minced green onion.

CHAPTER 3

NOODLES, FLOUR AND RICE

Dried Noodles, *Gan Mian* 干面

There is such a variety of dried noodles at Asian markets that it can be overwhelming. Most Asian markets group their noodles by ethnicity. In my local market, Chinese noodles have a separate aisle from Japanese and Korean noodles. The most common noodles in China are wheat noodles, *mian*面, made with wheat flour, water and salt. Rice noodles, or rice sticks, and sweet potato noodles are called *fen* 粉. Mung bean noodles are called *fensi* 粉丝.

Dried wheat noodles are cooked in boiling water without presoaking, but presoaking is needed for dried rice noodles, sweet potato noodles and mung bean noodles. If you use fresh or frozen noodles, no presoaking is needed. Any of the dried noodles can be found fresh or frozen in an Asian market. Below, you will find a guide for which kind of noodles to use in your dish.

Wheat Noodles面

Thin round noodles are also called *gua mian* or dragon whisker noodles. I like to use thin noodles for everyday noodle dishes because they absorb more flavor from the broth. Chinese and Japanese wheat noodles are similar, so you can use Japanese *somen* noodles in place of Chinese wheat noodles. Somen noodles are also good for Japanese ramen dishes.

Flat noodles are made with the same ingredients as thin round noodles but are wider and flatter. They are used in dishes such as Dan Dan Noodles (page 75).

Egg noodles are wheat noodles that contain eggs. They come packaged in straight lengths as well as tangled bunches. Egg noodles are used in many Cantonese dishes such as *lo mian, chow mian* and wonton noodle soup.

Udon noodles are the thickest noodles you can find at an Asian market and you can use them for noodle soup. *Tian shui mian* is a famous noodle dish from Sichuan with a spicy sauce over the noodles.

Buckwheat Noodles

Wheat Noodles in thinner shape

Egg Noodles

Wheat Noodles in wider shape

Sweet Potato Noodles

Mung Bean Noodles

Rice Noodles

Wheat Noodles

Rice Noodles 米线/米粉

The thin rice vermicelli noodles are the thinnest ones in this category and can be used in spring rolls, salads, soups and stir-fries. Medium-sized rice noodles are also called "rice sticks" on the label and are called *mi xian* in Chinese. I use this type of rice noodle for Rice Noodles with Pickled Mustard Greens (page 91) in Chapter 3. This medium-sized rice noodle is also suitable for Vietnamese *pho* and pad Thai. Both size rice noodles need to be soaked first, then boiled.

Mung Bean Noodles 绿豆粉丝

Mung bean noodles are sometimes called glass noodles. The Ants Climbing a Tree recipe (page 88) in this chapter uses this kind of noodle. They are small and thin and called glass noodles because the color is clear and transparent when they cook since they are made from mung bean starch. I use the **Double Pagoda** brand which says on the package "Lung Kuw Mung Bean Threads Noodle—Vermicelli." Mung bean noodles are used in soups, stir-fries and salads.

Sweet Potato Noodles 红薯粉

Sweet potato noodles are commonly used in China and are good for soups and stew dishes. The Hot and Sour Noodles recipe (page 84) in this chapter uses this kind of noodle. In Korea, sweet potato noodles are called glass noodles and stir-fried in sesame oil with meat and vegetables, a popular dish called *japchae*.

Buckwheat Noodles 荞麦面

Buckwheat noodles are called *qiao mai mian* in Chinese. These noodles are served in hot soup with spicy sauce in Sichuan. Buckwheat noodles are also served cold with vegetables. In Japan, buckwheat noodles are called *soba* noodles and are served chilled with a dipping sauce.

Rice, *Mi* 米

Rice is a big part of Chinese culture. If there is a meal without rice, it is not considered a complete meal. When I moved to the U.S. from China, the first thing I wanted to find was rice similar to the type I ate in China. After trying many brands, here are some tips on how to pick out rice at an Asian market.

In America, rice comes in long grain, medium grain and short grain. Long-grain rice is less sticky than short-grain rice. Medium-grain rice is the type similar to those we eat every day in China. When cooked, short-grain rice sticks together.

Xian Mi 籼米

Xian mi is white rice and comes in long or medium grain. The rice is usually served at a Thai restaurant as Jasmine rice or Indian restaurants as Basmati rice. I often buy the **Kokuho** brand. The Kokuho rice in the yellow packaging is good for everyday rice. Kokuho Rose in the red packaging has a softer texture and is good for everyday use and great for making congee. **Botan Calrose** and **Nishiki** are good brands too.

Gengmi 梗米

Also called Japonica rice, *gengmi* is smaller in size and is a short-grain rice. This rice is perfect for sushi making. The brands I like are **Shirakiku**, **Koshihikari** and **SEKKA**.

Nuomi 糯米

Nuomi is also called glutinous rice, or sweet rice. The best nuomi is from Sichuan. We use this kind of rice to make sticky rice dumplings and rice wine and also add it to congee. The brands I use here are **Apple Brand** and **Sho-Shiku-Bai**.

Brown rice 糙米

Brown rice is a whole grain rice with the inedible outer hull removed. You can cook brown rice mixed with white rice to eat with a meal and you may add brown rice to any congee. The brands I like are **Nishiki** and **Sukoyaka**.

Flours, *Mian Fen* 面粉

Wheat flour is used to make dumpling and wonton wrappers, buns, noodles and pancakes. I use all-purpose flour for all of these dishes.

Rice flour 粘米粉 is ground from long- or medium-grain rice and is used to make rice cakes and radish cakes. It is not as sticky as sweet rice.

Glutinous rice flour or sweet rice flour 糯米粉 is ground from sweet rice and used in desserts such as Japanese *mochi* (page 150) and Chinese *tang yuan*, or sweet rice balls.

Mung bean starch 绿豆粉 is made from mung beans and is used to make Sichuan "Jelly Noodles" (page 76) in this chapter. It is also used as a sauce thickener. For any recipe in this book, you can use mung bean starch in place of cornstarch for thickening sauces.

PORK AND CHIVE DUMPLINGS

Jiu Cai Jiao Zi 韭菜饺子

YIELDS 32 DUMPLINGS,
3 TO 4 SERVINGS

INGREDIENTS

DUMPLING WRAPPERS

2½ cups (313 g) all-purpose flour

1½ tsp (9 g) salt

About ¾ cup + 2 tsp (200 ml) water

FILLING

5¼ cups (250 g) Chinese chives, finely chopped

1 lb (450 g) ground pork

3 tsp (15 g) minced ginger

⅔ cup (64 g) chopped green onion

2 eggs

1 tsp cornstarch

1 tsp salt

2 tbsp (30 ml) Chinese soy sauce

1 tbsp (15 ml) Chinese cooking wine

1 tsp sesame oil

In China, there are restaurants that just sell dumplings. You can even buy raw dumplings from street vendors to cook at home. When I grew up, my family made our own dumplings with this filling. I apprenticed by learning how to roll the wrappers and wrap the dumplings. The store-bought wrappers are perfectly fine to use, but they are drier than the fresh wrappers, so you need to wet the edges in order to seal them. Freshly made wrappers have a chewier texture than frozen ones and combined with a juicy, fragrant filling, the delicious taste is far superior than store-bought frozen dumplings.

INSTRUCTIONS

To make the dumpling wrappers, add the flour and salt to the bowl of a stand mixer and using the dough hook attachment, turn to low speed. Gradually add the water to form a lumpy dough. Continue kneading on medium speed for 15 minutes. Remove the bowl from the mixer and cover with a damp cloth for 30 minutes.

Make the dumpling filling while waiting for the dough to rest. Place the Chinese chives and ground pork in a large bowl with the minced ginger, chopped green onion, eggs, cornstarch, salt, soy sauce, cooking wine and sesame oil. Using chopsticks, mix in one direction. You can also mix the filling in a stand mixer. Cover the bowl and chill in the refrigerator until you are ready to use it.

(continued)

DUMPLING SAUCE

3 cloves garlic, chopped

1 tbsp (15 ml) chili oil

1 tsp Sichuan peppercorn oil (page 112)

4 tbsp (60 ml) soy sauce

1 tbsp (15 ml) Chinese vinegar

½ tbsp (8 g) sugar

½ tsp salt

Put the rested dough on a flat surface and knead with your hands for a minute or two. The dough should be very smooth and elastic. Divide the dough into four parts and roll each part into a long rope shape. Divide each rope into eight pieces; each rope of dough should yield eight dumpling wrappers. Keep the pieces you are not working with covered. Using your hand, press a piece of dough into a small disc and while holding the edge of the disc with one hand, use a rolling pin in your other hand to flatten the dough, rotating the disc 30 degrees after each roll. Roll and turn, roll and turn. The wrappers should be thicker in the middle and thinner around the edges. After some practice, you can make them quite efficiently. Use the fresh wrappers immediately or freeze them. To freeze, sprinkle some flour in between each wrapper, stack and place them in an airtight bag. Take a wrapper and place 1 tablespoon (15 g) of filling in the center, fold over the edges of the wrapper and pinch closed. Holding the dumpling with both hands, crimp the top of the dumpling between your thumbs and index fingers. There are many different ways to crimp or pleat the dumplings, but this is the technique I learned from my grandmother.

Bring a large pot of water to a boil, add 1 tablespoon (18 g) of salt, then the dumplings. Do not crowd the pot with too many dumplings. Use the back of a ladle to stir the bottom of the pot to prevent the dumplings from sticking. When the pot boils again, add 1 cup (240 ml) of cold water. After it comes to a boil once again, cook for an additional 3 minutes and then remove the dumplings from the pot with a slotted spoon.

To make the dumpling sauce, mix the garlic, chili oil, Sichuan peppercorn oil, soy sauce, Chinese vinegar, sugar and salt in a small bowl and serve the dumplings hot with the sauce on the side.

FRESH HANDMADE CHINESE NOODLES

Shou Gong Mian 手工面

INGREDIENTS

2¼ cups (280 g) all-purpose flour, plus extra for rolling out the dough

¼ tsp salt

½–⅝ cup (120–145 ml) lukewarm water

Making fresh noodles at home requires some time and effort but is well worth it. Freshly cooked noodles have a superior taste and a chewier texture compared to store-bought dry noodles. They cook much faster than dried noodles. This recipe makes about two 5-ounce (150-g) portions of noodles, which you can use in my Dan Dan Noodles recipe (page 75). These fresh noodles are meant to be used the same day they are made, but you can toss extra flour on them, seal them in a ziplock and freeze them.

INSTRUCTIONS

Using a stand mixer, add the flour and salt to the bowl and attach a dough hook. Turn the mixer on low speed, then gradually add water, giving the flour time to absorb the water with each addition. Continue to mix the dough on medium speed for 5 minutes, at which point you should have a dough that appears shaggy. Continue to knead with the mixer for another 10 minutes. Cover the dough with a damp cloth and set aside to rest, covered, for 30 minutes.

After the dough has rested, knead the dough in the bowl with your hands a few times and form it into a ball. Sprinkle flour on a flat surface and place the dough on top. Cut the dough into two pieces. Cover one piece with a damp cloth and set aside. Roll the first piece of dough with a rolling pin into a rectangle shape about 2 millimeters thick. Flour the surface of the dough on both sides so it does not stick when you fold it. Grasp one of the narrower ends of the rectangle and fold the dough into four layers. Slice the noodles with a sharp knife to your desired thickness, about ⅛ inch (3 mm) thick.

Once the noodles are cut, separate them and sprinkle flour onto them so they do not stick together. Bring a large pot of water to a boil and add the noodles. When the water comes to a boil again, add ½ cup (120 ml) of cold water and let the pot come to a boil a second time. The total cooking time is 1 to 4 minutes depending on how thick the noodles are. Noodles that are ⅛ inch (3 mm) thick should be done in about 2 minutes. These fresh noodles can be used with many noodle dishes, such as sesame noodles, sweet bean paste noodles and beef noodle soup.

DAN DAN
NOODLES

Dan Dan Mian 担担面

YIELDS 1 SERVING

INGREDIENTS

SAUCE

3 tbsp (45 ml) soy sauce

1 tbsp (15 ml) Chinese vinegar

2–3 tsp (10–15 ml) Sichuan chili oil

¼ tsp Sichuan peppercorn powder

1 tbsp (6 g) chopped green onion

1 tsp melted lard

1 tbsp (9 g) roasted crushed peanuts, plus more for garnish

2 tbsp (30 ml) hot gao tang (page 40) or hot water

Salt, to taste

MEAT TOPPING

2 tbsp (30 ml) cooking oil

2 oz (57 g) ground pork

1 star anise

1 tbsp (15 ml) Chinese cooking wine

1 tbsp (15 g) preserved vegetable (ya cai)

5 oz (142 g) fresh handmade noodles (page 72) or 3 oz (80 g) dried Chinese noodles, cooked

Everyone has heard of, if not eaten, Dan Dan noodles. The name, *"Dan Dan"* means "carrying a pole," or *bian dan* in Chinese. This is because when this noodle dish was a street food, the seller would use a carrying pole to carry a small stove on one end and the noodles and seasoning on the other. He would walk around town calling out the name of the noodle dish, *"Dan Dan Mian,"* and people would come over to buy a bowl. This classic Sichuan noodle dish is served in a spicy soy and vinegar sauce, then topped with stir-fried pork and ya cai. You can add a boiled leafy vegetable as well. In American Chinese restaurants, the soy and vinegar sauce is often replaced with a sweet sesame sauce.

INSTRUCTIONS

Put the soy sauce, Chinese vinegar, Sichuan chili oil, Sichuan peppercorn powder, chopped green onion, melted lard and roasted crushed peanuts into a noodle bowl, add the hot gao tang and salt and mix everything together. Heat the cooking oil over medium-high, add the ground pork and star anise and stir-fry. After 30 seconds, add the cooking wine and cook until the pork is opaque, about 2 minutes. Add the ya cai and stir-fry for about 3 minutes, or until the pork is crispy brown. Put the mixture in a small bowl and set aside.

Drain the cooked handmade noodles and place them in the noodle bowl with the sauce. Sprinkle the meat mixture on top of the noodles and add some crushed peanuts for garnish. Serve hot and before eating, mix the meat topping, noodles and sauce with chopsticks until the sauce and the meat are evenly distributed.

SICHUAN "JELLY NOODLES"

Sichuan Liang Fen
四川凉粉

YIELDS 4 SERVINGS

INGREDIENTS

JELLY NOODLE MIXTURE

1 cup (135 g) mung bean starch

6 cups (1.4 L) water, divided

SAUCE

1 tbsp (8 g) Sichuan chili powder

¼ tsp Sichuan peppercorn powder

1 tbsp (15 g) minced garlic

1 tbsp (15 ml) cooking oil

1 tsp salt

1 tbsp (15 g) sugar

2 tbsp (30 ml) soy sauce

2 tbsp (30 ml) Chinese vinegar

1 tbsp (6 g) chopped green onion, for garnish

There is no jelly in these noodles and they are not what Western people consider to be a noodle. "Jelly noodles" are made from a mixture of mung bean starch and water. The mixture is poured into a rectangular container and placed in the refrigerator to thicken into a gelatin-like consistency. Then it is cut into noodle shapes or cubes. It's a dish with an interesting texture and wonderful savory, spicy and pungent flavors.

INSTRUCTIONS

In a medium bowl, mix the mung bean starch with 1 cup (240 ml) of water and mix well until the starch has dissolved. Add 5 cups (1.2 L) of water to a pot and bring to a boil. Gradually add the mung bean mixture to the boiling water and keep stirring with a spatula until the mixture thickens. Pour the mixture into an 8 x 8–inch (20 x 20–cm) container or 9-inch (23-cm) bread pan—depending upon the jelly noodle shape you want—cover and place in the refrigerator for 1 hour until firm.

While the mixture is in the refrigerator, make the sauce. In a heatproof bowl, add the chili powder, Sichuan peppercorn powder and garlic. In a wok or small pan, heat the cooking oil over high heat until smoking. Remove the wok from the heat source and let it cool for 15 seconds. Then pour the oil over the spices, add the remaining sauce ingredients and mix well. Take the block of noodles out of the pan and place on a cutting board. Cut into long noodle shapes or cubes. Transfer the jelly noodles to a serving dish and pour the sauce over them. Garnish with green onion and serve cold or at room temperature.

STEAMED BUNS
FILLED WITH PORK AND PRESERVED VEGETABLE

Ya Cai Bao Zi 芽菜包子

YIELDS 10-12 BUNS

INGREDIENTS

DOUGH

1½ tsp (4 g) instant yeast

1¼ cups (300 ml) lukewarm water, divided

1 tsp sugar

4 cups (500 g) all-purpose flour

2 tsp (8 g) lard, melted

1 tsp salt

FILLING

3 tbsp (45 ml) cooking oil

1 lb (450 g) ground pork

2 tbsp (30 ml) Chinese cooking wine

9 tbsp (135 g) preserved vegetable (ya cai)

¾ cup (150 g) bamboo, chopped

1 tbsp (15 g) sugar

Steamed buns are ubiquitous in China and there are many regional fillings. Probably the most well known in the West is *char siu bao*, or barbecue pork buns, from Hong Kong (China). My recipe is a Sichuan version. The filling is made from Sichuan *ya cai* stir-fried with pork and bamboo. The ya cai adds a distinct Sichuan pickle flavor and the bamboo adds a crunchy texture to the filling.

INSTRUCTIONS

In a small bowl, proof the yeast in 1 cup (240 ml) of lukewarm water and sugar for 15 minutes or until the liquid starts to foam. Place the flour and yeast mixture in the bowl of a stand mixer and add ¼ cup (60 ml) of lukewarm water, lard and salt. Using the dough hook, knead on medium speed for 10 minutes. Then, place the dough in an oiled bowl, cover with a damp cloth and let rise for about 2 hours, until it doubles in size. Push it down and set aside for another 15 minutes.

While you are waiting for the dough to rise, make the filling. Heat the wok over high heat, add the cooking oil and stir-fry the ground pork for 30 seconds. Next, add the cooking wine and stir-fry until the pork is opaque. Add the ya cai and bamboo and stir-fry until the pork is a little crispy and brown. Add the sugar, mix, then transfer the filling to a container to cool. Place the filling in the refrigerator for at least 1 hour. Cooling the filling will make wrapping the buns much easier. You can make the filling a day in advance.

Divide the dough into four equal pieces, then cut each large piece into 2-ounce (60-g) portions. Cover the dough you are not working with. Take a 2-ounce (60-g) piece of dough, lay it on a flat, floured surface and press it down. Using a rolling pin, roll the dough into a 5-inch (13-cm) round shape. This recipe can make about 10 to 12 buns. Place 2 tablespoons (30 g) of filling in the middle of the wrapper. Hold the wrapper with the filling in the palm of one hand and with the thumb and index finger of your other hand, seal the opposing edges of the dough in a clockwise direction, making pleats as you seal the bun. Cut some wax paper into squares big enough to cover the bottom of each bun so the buns will not stick to the bottom of the steamer. Place each bun on a piece of wax paper, let the buns rise again on steamer trays for 15 minutes, then place the trays in a steamer for 10 to 12 minutes. The bun filling should be heated thoroughly and the bun should have a spongy feel.

CHINESE SCALLION PANCAKES

Cong You Bing 葱油饼

YIELDS 5 SERVINGS

INGREDIENTS

2 cups (250 g) all-purpose flour

¼ tsp salt

15 tbsp + 2 tsp (100 ml) hot water

3–4 tbsp (45–60 ml) cold water

3 tbsp (45 ml) cooking oil, for frying, and 1 tbsp (15 ml) for brushing the pancakes

1 green onion, chopped

These wheat flour pancakes are filled with green onion and rolled out into layers before panfrying. They are crispy on the outside and chewy inside with a mild onion flavor. They are often eaten for breakfast or with congee. Serve them hot or at room temperature.

INSTRUCTIONS

Place the flour and salt in the bowl of a stand mixer and using the dough hook attachment on low speed, gradually add the hot water. The dough will be a little dry. Turn the mixer speed to medium and add the cold water a little at a time until you have a smooth dough. Remove the bowl from the mixer and cover with plastic wrap. Rest the dough at room temperature for 30 minutes.

Roll the dough into a log and divide it into five parts. Take one piece and cover the others with a damp cheesecloth or plastic wrap. Press the dough flat with your palm and then using a rolling pin, roll it into a rectangular shape about ⅛ inch (3 mm) thick. Brush a little cooking oil evenly across the surface of the flattened dough and then sprinkle some of the chopped green onion on top.

Starting from one of the longer ends, roll the dough into a cigar shape with the green onion wrapped inside. Next, starting from one of the short ends of the cigar shape, roll it up again like you would a cinnamon roll. Cover the dough with plastic wrap and let it rest for 10 minutes. Repeat with the other four pieces of dough. After the dough has rested, take one roll and lay it on its side. Using a rolling pin, flatten it into a pancake shape. Heat a frying pan over medium heat and add the cooking oil. Fry the pancakes over medium heat for about 3 minutes or until golden brown on both sides. Serve immediately so that the pancakes are crispy on the outside.

MUNG BEAN **CONGEE**

Lu Dou Xi Fan 绿豆稀饭

Congees can be made with a variety of beans, vegetables, meat or seafood. This mung bean congee is a simple vegetarian dish. It can be eaten with any meal. If eaten for dinner, it is served with a variety of side dishes such as scallion pancakes (page 80) and pickles.

YIELDS 6 SERVINGS

INGREDIENTS

¼ cup (60 g) dried mung beans

1 cup (200 g) white rice

2½ quarts (2.4 L) water, divided

½ cup (118 g) sticky rice (sweet rice)

INSTRUCTIONS

Wash the mung beans and rice and place them in a large pot. Add half of the water and bring to a boil. Once boiling, cook the beans for 5 minutes. Add the sticky rice and remaining water to the pot and stir to mix. Bring to a boil and then reduce the heat to low. Cover the pot and cook until the beans and rice are the consistency of oatmeal, 45 minutes to 1 hour. Stir occasionally in the first 30 minutes, then frequently during the last 20 minutes of cooking to prevent the congee from sticking to the bottom. After it is cooked, the congee will continue to thicken as it stands. Thin it with water as needed. This dish is usually served in a bowl and eaten with buns or scallion pancakes (page 86).

HOT AND SOUR SWEET POTATO NOODLES

Suan La Fen 酸辣粉

YIELDS 1 SERVING

INGREDIENTS

5 oz (142 g) sweet potato noodles

⅝ cup (60 g) dry soybeans

1 cup (240 ml) cooking oil

10 tbsp (150 ml) gao tang (page 40) or hot water

NOODLE SEASONING

2 tsp (10 g) minced garlic

¼ tsp Sichuan peppercorn powder or oil

¼ tsp salt

2 tbsp (30 ml) vinegar

1½ tbsp (23 ml) soy sauce

½ tbsp (8 ml) chili oil plus 1 tsp sediment from the chili oil jar

2 tsp (8 g) lard (optional)

NOODLE TOPPING

1 tbsp (6 g) chopped green onion

2 tbsp (30 g) preserved mustard stems

2 tbsp (13 g) chopped celery

This sweet potato dish is a popular street food in Sichuan. The vendor puts the noodles in a bowl and adds the sauce and toppings one by one in front of you. A famous version of this dish includes boiled pork intestine. The sauce packs the silky potato noodles with spicy, numbing, sour and umami flavor. The fried soybean topping adds a crunchy texture and more complex flavor. Instead of sweet potato noodles, you can make this dish with buckwheat noodles, which have a chewy texture and a nutty flavor.

INSTRUCTIONS

Soak the sweet potato noodles in warm water for 30 minutes, or you can soak them in cold water overnight. Also soak the soybeans in warm water for 2 hours or overnight.

To make the fried soybean topping, heat the cooking oil to 260°F (125°C) and add the soaked soybeans (dry them with a paper towel before frying them). Keep the oil temperature between 260 and 320°F (125 and 160°C) and fry the beans for about 8 minutes until they are golden brown.

Then, bring a large pot of water to a boil, drain the noodles and place them in the boiling water. Boil them for about 2 minutes and then transfer the noodles to a bowl of ice water. Heat the gao tang just until boiling. Drain the noodles from the ice water and place them in a noodle bowl.

To make the noodle seasoning, combine the minced garlic, Sichuan peppercorn powder, salt, vinegar, soy sauce, chili oil with some of the sediment and, if you wish, the lard. Pour on top of the noodles and then prepare the topping by combining the chopped green onion, preserved mustard stems, chopped celery and fried soybeans. Pour the topping mixture over the noodles, followed by the hot gao tang. Serve hot and mix all the ingredients with the noodles before eating.

DRAGON
WONTONS

Long Chao Shou 龙抄手

YIELDS 40 WONTONS

INGREDIENTS

WONTONS

4 oz (113 g) ginger, minced

½ cup (120 ml) cold water

1 lb (454 g) ground pork

3 tbsp (45 ml) cooking wine

2 tsp (10 ml) sesame oil

1 tsp salt

2 eggs

1 package square wonton wrappers

SOUP FOR ONE

1½ cups (360 ml) chicken broth (homemade or store-bought)

Salt, to taste

Pinch of white pepper powder

1 tbsp (4 g) lard or sesame oil (optional, but really adds flavor)

½ cup (120 ml) cold water

1 tsp chopped green onion, for garnish

This is a very famous version of wonton soup from a restaurant in Sichuan named Long Chao Shou. The soup is served with a variety of small side dishes. A bowl of this wonton soup is the best comfort food because it brings me back to when I was a child, eating this soup with my grandma. The hot aromatic broth is warm and soothing and tastes just like home.

Any uncooked wontons can be frozen for later use. Sprinkle some flour on a baking pan, then lay the wontons on the pan and place the pan in the freezer. Once they are frozen, transfer them to a plastic freezer bag. You can use them for up to 2 months.

INSTRUCTIONS

In a small bowl, soak the minced ginger in the cold water for 15 minutes. Then, drain the water into a cup, reserving the ginger water for the filling. In a medium-sized mixing bowl, add the pork, cooking wine, sesame oil, salt and eggs. Mix well, then add ¼ cup (60 ml) of ginger water and combine the ingredients. Put a tablespoon (15 g) of the pork filling in the center of a wonton wrapper. Fold the wonton in half diagonally to create a triangle and seal the edges. Fold the two opposing corners in on each other and press again to seal. The folded wonton will have a boat shape. Repeat until all the wonton wrappers are filled.

Heat the chicken broth and add salt, white pepper and lard (if using), then pour the soup base into a bowl and set aside. Bring a pot of water to a boil. Add the wontons one at a time to the pot. Then use a ladle to swirl around the wontons to prevent them from sticking to the bottom. When the water boils again, add the cold water, return to a boil and cook another 1 to 2 minutes. Do not overcook them. Remove the wontons with a slotted spoon and put them in the prepared chicken soup bowl. Garnish with green onion and serve.

ANTS CLIMBING A TREE

(MUNG BEAN NOODLES WITH GROUND PORK)

Ma Yi Shang Shu

蚂蚁上树

YIELDS 4 SERVINGS

INGREDIENTS

10 oz (282 g) dried mung bean noodles

3 tbsp (45 ml) cooking oil

5 oz (142 g) ground pork

1 green onion, chopped

1 tbsp (6 g) chopped ginger

2 tbsp (30 g) chopped garlic

1 tsp chopped pickled chili peppers

3 tbsp (45 g) Sichuan broad bean chili paste (dou ban)

10 tbsp (150 ml) gao tang (page 40) or hot water

1 green onion, minced, for garnish

This Sichuan dish gets its name from the appearance of the meat sticking to the noodles. The mung bean noodles represent tree branches; the chopped scallions represent the tree leaves; and the little bits of ground meat represent the ants. It consists of mung bean noodles covered with a very spicy pork sauce. Dou ban gives the dish its spicy Sichuan flavor; the pickled chili peppers intensify the heat and add a tanginess to the sauce. The mung bean noodles absorb the liquid very quickly, so you can add more stock to the dish before serving.

INSTRUCTIONS

In a large bowl, soak the dried noodles in hot water for 5 minutes, then drain. Heat the cooking oil in a wok over high heat until smoking. Then add the ground pork and stir-fry until the pork loses its pink color, for about 2 minutes. Add the green onion, ginger, garlic and pickled peppers, stir-frying until fragrant.

Turn the heat down to medium, add the dou ban and stir-fry for about 1 minute or until you see that the oil has turned red. Add the noodles to the wok and mix well. Finally, pour in the gao tang or hot water and continue to cook over high heat until the gao tang cooks down. Serve hot and garnish with minced green onion.

RICE NOODLES
WITH PICKLED MUSTARD GREENS

Suan Cai Mi Xian
酸菜米线

YIELDS 1 SERVING

INGREDIENTS

4 oz (113 g) dried rice noodles

2 tbsp (30 ml) cooking oil

4 oz (113 g) ground pork or chopped mushroom (for a vegan option)

1 tbsp (15 ml) cooking wine

3 cloves garlic, chopped

6 dried red chili peppers

7½ tbsp (113 g) pickled mustard greens (suan cai), chopped into small pieces

1½ cups (360 ml) chicken stock or warm water

¼ tsp salt

¼ tsp white pepper powder

1 tbsp (15 ml) Chinese vinegar

½ tsp chicken bouillon

1 tbsp (6 g) green onion, minced, for garnish

Suan cai are usually paired with rice noodles, which are gluten free. Rice noodles retain a fresh rice taste with a springy texture and do not get mushy, but you can substitute any type of noodle you like. The pickled mustard greens add a crunchy texture and tangy flavor to the rice noodles. Pickled chili peppers are often used in this dish, but my version uses dried red chili peppers because they are easier to find in western Asian markets.

INSTRUCTIONS

In a large bowl, soak the rice noodles in hot water for 1 hour until soft, then drain. Heat a wok over medium-high heat, then add the cooking oil.

Once the oil is hot, add the ground pork and stir-fry for 10 seconds. Add the cooking wine and continue to stir-fry until opaque, for about 1 minute. Add the garlic and dried chili peppers and stir-fry until they release their fragrance. Then, add the pickled mustard greens and stir-fry with the pork for about 30 seconds. Add the chicken stock, salt, white pepper powder, vinegar and chicken bouillon to the wok and bring to a boil. Once boiling, place the noodles in the liquid. Cook for 3 minutes and serve garnished with green onion.

CHAPTER 4

DRY SPICES

Dried Chili Peppers, *Gan La Jiao* 干辣椒

In Sichuan, the two most popular hot red peppers are called *erjingtiao* and *qixingjiao*. Erjingtiao is a long, thin, mild pepper with a curved tail. They are used fresh to make dou ban, or broad bean chili paste, and can also be pickled or dried. Qixiangjiao is one variety of "heaven facing" peppers named for how the peppers point towards the sky while on the plant and are found in many Asian markets outside of China. They are much shorter and smaller than erjingtiao. In general, the smaller the chili, the hotter it is. They are sold as dried whole peppers and ground hot pepper powder. This pepper is great for making chili oil. Look at the package label for brands coming from the Sichuan region of China. Western peppers and Sichuan peppers differ in flavor and color. This makes a huge difference in the quality and flavor of the chili oil!

Korean red chili powder is cayenne pepper powder and has a different flavor from Sichuan chili peppers. The variety used in Korean chili powder is milder and slightly sweeter than Sichuan hot peppers. Sichuan chili peppers are much hotter and have a spicy aroma. In my kimchi recipe (page 31), I use Korean red chili powder. I once used Sichuan chili powder and it turned out much spicier than any kimchi I have ever eaten.

Sichuan Peppercorns, *Sichuan Hua Jiao* 花椒

One of the most important ingredients in Sichuan cuisine is Sichuan peppercorns, *hua jiao,* known for the numbing and tingling sensation they produce on the tongue. They're actually seed husks, not peppercorns, and are fragrant and lemony. Sichuan peppercorns can be used whole or ground into powder. There are red Sichuan peppercorns, which are used in a variety of dishes, as well as green peppercorns, called "green flower pepper." This variety has a fresh lime peel aroma and is perfect for fish dishes. The best Sichuan peppercorns grow in Hanyuan County in western Sichuan and are called *gongjiao. Gong* means "imperial quality" and *jiao* is the Sichuan peppercorn. In imperial China, gongjiao were produced only for the Chinese emperor.

When you are buying Sichuan peppercorns in an Asian market, look for the brands imported from Sichuan. Better yet, if you can find a brand from Hanyuan, you have found China's finest-quality hua jiao.

Sichuan peppercorns have an extremely short shelf life. Many of the ones you see in an Asian market have been sitting on the shelf for too long and have lost much of their fragrance and numbing quality. Look at the date on the packaging and try to buy a small package that will not sit for too long on your shelf.

Sichuan peppercorns begin to lose their flavor shortly after they are ground, so the best method is to buy whole peppercorns and grind them as needed. If you buy Sichuan peppercorn powder, use it as quickly as possible, or use it to make Sichuan peppercorn oil, which can preserve the aroma for much longer. I vacuum seal Sichuan peppercorns in small packs to lengthen their shelf life.

Star Anise, *Ba Jiao* 八角

Star anise is the seed pod from the fruit of the *Illicium verum* plant, an evergreen shrub native to Southwest China. The English name refers to its star shape. The Chinese name is *ba jiao*. *Ba* means the number eight and *jao* means angle or corner. Each star anise has eight pointed angles. This spice is widely used in braises, stews and soups. It is one of the main flavors in Chinese five spice powder.

Five Spice Powder, *Wu Xiang Fen* 五香粉

Five spice powder is a spice mixture of Sichuan peppercorns, fennel seeds, star anise, cinnamon and cloves. Some varieties add additional spices. One famous variety is called *shisanxiang*, a mixture of 13 spices. Any variety of the different spice powders can be used in many meat dishes as a spice rub for pork, chicken and seafood, in red-cooked recipes, or any fried-food breading. I add five spice powder to Korean fried chicken breading to add a more complex aroma to the dish. I usually buy five spice powder in a small bottle because it is easier to store and preserve the aroma.

Sesame Seeds, *Zhi Ma* 芝麻

Sesame is a flowering plant with edible seeds that grow in pods. Chinese recipes also feature the seeds after they have been toasted and blended into a paste as well as made into an oil. There are black, tan or brown and white sesame seeds. The black ones have a stronger rich nutty flavor. The pure white sesame seeds have had the hull removed and have a milder nutty flavor. Some unhulled sesame seeds still have a white, tan or off-white color, making them difficult to distinguish from hulled sesame seeds. Examine the packaging to determine whether they are hulled or unhulled.

Cassia Bark, *Gui Pi* 桂皮

Cassia bark, or Chinese cinnamon, comes from the bark of the *cinnamomum* cassia tree, which originated in Southern China. It has a long history in Chinese cooking and traditional Chinese medicine. It has a dark brown to red color and is sold as thick sticks. Cassia cinnamon is the most common variety found in Asian markets. Another kind of cinnamon, Ceylon cinnamon, is native to Sri Lanka and southern India. It is more expensive than Chinese cinnamon and has a milder aroma and flavor. It is often labeled "Ceylon cinnamon" on the packaging. Store ground cinnamon or cinnamon sticks in an airtight container in a cool, dark place. As with all ground spices, it is best to buy them in small quantities as they quickly lose their flavor and aroma.

Bay Leaves, *Yu Gui Ye* 月桂叶

Bay leaves are popular in Chinese cooking, especially in meat dishes. They come from the laurel tree, *laurus nobilis*, an aromatic evergreen tree. When added to stews, roasts or sauces, they slowly release their flavor. The longer you cook them, the more they produce their floral and savory flavor. The leaves can be crushed or ground before cooking and are generally removed from the dish before serving.

Dried Orange Peel, *Chen Pi* 陈皮

Orange peel, *chen pi* in Chinese, is a sun-dried mandarin orange peel used in Chinese cooking and traditional medicine. It is dry aged and the older, the better. I use it in many cooked red meat dishes. It can be infused into a marinade or syrup and brushed on chicken or duck before roasting. It gives the dish a citrus flavor and gives the food a refreshing taste. You can also use dried orange peel as an herbal tea. Fresh peels are not considered to have the same medicinal effects as dried peels and as such are not considered suitable for drinking as a tea.

CHINESE MASTER BRAISING SAUCE

Lu Shui 卤水

YIELDS ABOUT 3 QUARTS (3 L)

INGREDIENTS

About 12 star anise (10 g)

About 5 cinnamon sticks (10 g)

4 tsp (8 g) fennel seeds

2 tbsp (8 g) sand ginger

5 tsp (10 g) Sichuan peppercorns

2½ tsp (8 g) dried orange peel

4 Chinese black cardamom pods

1 tbsp (7 g) green cardamom pods

6 bay leaves

1 tbsp (9 g) cloves

3⅔ tbsp (55 ml) cooking oil

5⅔ tbsp (85 g) rock sugar

2 cups (480 ml) hot water

3 quarts (2.9 L) pork or chicken stock

9⅓ tbsp (140 ml) light soy sauce

11⅔ tbsp (175 ml) dark soy sauce

9⅓ tbsp (56 g) fresh ginger, peeled and crushed

6 green onions (tie the roots in a knot)

2 tsp (12 g) salt

This sauce is used for Sichuan Braised Beef Slices, *Wu Xiang Niu Rou* (page 100) and has a deep, complex umami flavor from using many dried spices like star anise, cinnamon, fennel and dried orange peel. The sauce is reusable and tastes better with age. After using, filter the sauce and pour it into a container. You can store the sauce in the refrigerator for up to a week, or in the freezer for up to 3 months. Let it defrost in the refrigerator before bringing it to a boil. Add more water, stock and spices as needed. The sauce can be used on different cooked meats such as pork shoulder, chicken and chicken feet. Eggs smoked in this sauce are delicious.

INSTRUCTIONS

Combine the star anise, cinnamon sticks, fennel seeds, sand ginger, Sichuan peppercorns, dried orange peel, black (caoguo) and green cardamom pods, bay leaves and cloves, then put the spice mixture in one or two cheesecloth bags or disposable tea filter bags and set aside.

Heat the cooking oil in a wok over high heat, add the rock sugar and stir for about 2 minutes, or until the sugar has melted and caramelized into a dark brown color. Be sure to watch carefully to avoid burning the syrup. Turn the heat off and let the sugar cool for a couple of minutes. Carefully add the hot water. Do not add the water while the oil is very hot because it will splatter. After adding the water, turn the heat to medium. Add the pork stock, both soy sauces, ginger, green onions, salt and spice bags and bring to a boil for 15 minutes. The sauce is now ready to use for braising any meat.

BRAISED
PORK
BELLY

Hong Shao Rou 红烧肉

YIELDS 4 SERVINGS

INGREDIENTS

4 lb (1.8 kg) pork belly

3 tbsp (45 g) sugar

4–5 slices ginger

2 green onions, cut into 2-inch (5-cm) pieces, plus 2 more, minced, for garnish

4 star anise

2 bay leaves

1 tsp Sichuan peppercorns

⅓ cup (80 ml) cooking wine

¼ cup (60 ml) light soy sauce

1 tbsp (15 ml) dark soy sauce

2 cups (480 ml) hot water

This was one of my mother's signature dishes and one of my favorite dishes during my childhood—I loved to eat rice mixed with the sauce. This is the homestyle version of a famous dish called *Dongpo rou*, named after a famous poet. The main difference is that in Dongpo rou, the pork belly is cut into thick slices with the skin left on and braised in a casserole. This dish has a deep color from the dark soy sauce and a fragrant aroma from the star anise. Rice is a must-have with this dish!

INSTRUCTIONS

Cut the pork belly into 1-inch (2.5-cm)-thick pieces. Traditionally, the pork is boiled in water for a few minutes, then drained before stir-frying, but my method is easier. After cutting the pork, put it in a hot wok and stir-fry over medium heat until most of the fat is rendered. Pour the fat into a container and save as lard.

Stir-fry the pork with the remaining fat in the wok over medium heat for a few seconds, and then add the sugar and stir-fry until caramelized, about 2 minutes. Add the ginger, green onions, star anise, bay leaves and Sichuan peppercorns and stir-fry until fragrant. Add the cooking wine, light soy sauce and dark soy sauce, taking care to mix well. Add the hot water (enough to submerge the meat), and then cover the wok with a lid and simmer over low heat for 40 minutes. After about 40 minutes, the sauce should have thickened. Discard the bay leaves and serve hot, garnished with the minced green onion. This dish is also great served over rice.

SICHUAN BRAISED BEEF SLICES

Wu Xiang Lu Niu Rou
五香卤牛肉

YIELDS 4 TO 6 SERVINGS

INGREDIENTS

2½ lb (1.1 kg) beef brisket

1 tsp salt

3 quarts (3 L) Chinese Master Braising Sauce (page 96)

DIPPING POWDER

1 tbsp (5 g) Sichuan chili pepper powder

½ tsp Sichuan peppercorn powder

¼ tsp salt

¼ tsp chicken bouillon

This dish is served at room temperature, traditionally as a snack to accompany *bai jiu,* which is Chinese alcohol made with sorghum, wheat, barley and other grains. This dish also pairs well with vodka, as bai jiu is very similar. The beef is cooked in the Chinese Master Braising Sauce, *Lu Shui* (page 96), and the slices are dipped in a spicy dried powder mixture.

INSTRUCTIONS

Cut the beef brisket in half, rub with the salt and let sit for 30 minutes. Place the beef in a pot, add enough cold water to cover it by 2 inches (5 cm) and bring the water to a boil. As soon as the water boils, drain and rinse the meat with cold water.

Using the same pot, bring the Chinese Master Braising Sauce to a boil and add the beef brisket. After the liquid returns to a boil, reduce the heat to low and simmer for 60 to 90 minutes. To test for doneness, poke a chopstick into the center of the brisket. It should easily glide through the meat. Remove the brisket and let it rest until cool, then cut into ¼-inch (6-mm) slices. To make the dipping powder, mix together the Sichuan chili pepper powder, Sichuan peppercorn powder, salt and chicken bouillon in a small dish and serve alongside the sliced beef.

MALA
CHICKEN

La Zi Ji 辣子鸡

YIELDS 4 SERVINGS

INGREDIENTS

1 lb (454 g) boneless chicken thighs

¼ tsp white pepper powder

3 tbsp (45 ml) Shaoxing cooking wine, divided

1¼ tsp salt, divided

2–3 slices thinly sliced peeled ginger

2 oz (60 g) dried whole chili peppers

2 cups (480 ml) cooking oil

1½ tbsp (23 g) Sichuan broad bean chili paste (dou ban)

2⅓ tbsp (14 g) sliced ginger (5–6 slices)

1 tbsp (15 g) sliced garlic (4–5 cloves)

3 green onions, 2 cut into 2-inch (5-cm)-long pieces, 1 finely chopped

3½ tsp (7 g) Sichuan peppercorns

½ tsp sugar

2 tsp (6 g) sesame seeds

1 tsp sesame oil

This is a classic Sichuan dish from Chongqing. Traditionally, the chicken is cut up into small pieces with the bones. The crunchy fried chicken is served mixed into a large bed of stir-fried chili peppers, which gives off a very spicy aroma. The Sichuan peppercorns add a mouth-numbing sensation and the dish is served with an abundance of chili peppers covering the chicken. Digging around the dish with your chopsticks to find the chicken is half the fun of eating it.

INSTRUCTIONS

Cut the chicken into 2- to 3-inch (5- to 7.5-cm) cubes and place in a small bowl. To make the marinade, combine the white pepper powder, 2 tablespoons (30 ml) of cooking wine, 1 teaspoon of salt and 2 to 3 ginger slices. Pour over the chicken and marinate for 15 minutes. Cut all the dried chilis in half and shake out the seeds.

Heat the cooking oil in a wok over high heat to 350°F (175°C) and fry the marinated chicken for 3 to 4 minutes until brown. Remove the chicken with a slotted spoon to a plate and reheat the oil to 375°F (190°C). Return the chicken to the wok and stir-fry again for about 2 minutes or until golden brown. Take the chicken out with a slotted spoon. Pour out most of the extra oil, leaving about 3 tablespoons (45 ml) of oil in the wok.

Heat the oil over medium heat, add the dou ban and stir-fry until the oil turns red, about 1 minute. Add the ginger, garlic and the green onions cut into long pieces and stir-fry a few times. Then, add the dried chili peppers and Sichuan peppercorns and continue to stir-fry until fragrant, 2 to 3 minutes. Add the fried chicken back into the wok and mix with the fried spices. Add the remaining cooking wine, ¼ teaspoon of salt and the sugar. Finally, add the sesame seeds, stir-fry a few times, then add the sesame oil and chopped green onion. Stir-fry until everything is mixed well, then serve hot.

STEAMED PORK BELLY
WITH RICE POWDER

Fen Zheng Rou 粉蒸肉

YIELDS 4 SERVINGS

INGREDIENTS

9 tbsp (113 g) white rice

5 tbsp (56 g) sweet rice

4 tsp (8 g) Sichuan peppercorns, divided

2 star anise

1 bay leaf

5 dried chili peppers

1 lb (454 g) pork belly

½ tsp five spice powder

1 tbsp (15 ml) light soy sauce

1 tbsp (15 ml) dark soy sauce

1 tbsp (15 ml) cooking wine

1 tbsp (15 ml) fermented tofu water and a piece of the tofu

2 green onions, chopped, divided

1 tbsp (20 g) sweet flour paste

1 tbsp (6 g) chopped ginger

¾ lb (340 g) sweet potatoes

1 (3.5-oz ([100-g]) package rice powder mix

My grandmother always made this dish during Chinese New Year. Back then, it was a once-per-year treat for me. This dish dates back more than 2,000 years to the Zhou dynasty. During that time, it was served at royal banquets and the meat was steamed over lotus leaves instead of sweet potatoes. The pork is marinated in more than ten different spices and seasonings including five spice powder, then coated with rice powder. It is a great dish to serve at a dinner party, as it will surprise your guests when you open the steamer. The aromatic smell of all the spices in this dish is incredible. You can also use pork ribs or beef for this dish.

INSTRUCTIONS

Wash the white and sweet rice together and drain well. Roast the rice and 3½ teaspoons (7 g) of the Sichuan peppercorns in the oven at 350°F (175°C) for 15 minutes until slightly brown, or roast them in a wok or pan on a stove until brown. In a food processor, combine with the star anise, bay leaf and dried chili peppers and process into a powder.

Cut the pork belly into 3 x 5–inch (7.5 x 12.5–cm) strips that are ½ inch (1 cm) thick and then place the meat into a bowl. To make the marinade, grind the remaining ½ teaspoon of Sichuan peppercorns into small pieces and combine with the five spice powder, light and dark soy sauces, cooking wine, fermented tofu water and single piece of tofu, half of the chopped green onions, flour paste and chopped ginger. Pour the marinade over the meat, mix well and let sit for 20 minutes. Wash and cut the sweet potatoes lengthwise into ½-inch (1-cm)-thick, flat pieces and use them to line the bottom of a bamboo steamer. When you are ready to cook the dish, add the rice powder to the marinated meat and mix well. Lay the meat pieces on top of the sweet potatoes and steam over high heat for 1 hour or until the meat is tender. Serve hot and garnish with the remaining chopped green onions.

BRAISED BEEF STEW

WITH RADISH

Lou Bo Shao Niu Rou

萝卜烧牛肉

YIELDS 4 TO 6 SERVINGS

INGREDIENTS

1½ lb (680 g) beef brisket

5 cups (1.2 L) hot water

¼ cup (60 ml) soy sauce

½ tsp salt

3 tbsp (45 ml) Chinese cooking wine

2 green onions, cut into 2-inch (5-cm) pieces

4 star anise

1 bay leaf

3 tbsp (45 ml) canola oil

4 tbsp (60 g) Sichuan broad bean chili paste (dou ban)

1-inch (2.5-cm) piece ginger, peeled and crushed with a knife

½ tsp Sichuan peppercorns

3 cups (454 g) daikon radish, cut into 3-inch (8-cm) pieces

2 sprigs cilantro

Rice, for serving

This is a homestyle beef stew sometimes found on menus at small neighborhood restaurants. If you do not care for radish, you can substitute potatoes. The beef is soft and tender with a unique deep flavor from star anise, bay leaf and Sichuan peppercorns. The Sichuan broad bean chili paste adds a mild spicy flavor and the radish adds a crunchy texture to the dish. You can eat the stew right away, but stews always taste better reheated the next day.

INSTRUCTIONS

Cut the beef into 2-inch (5-cm) cubes and place in a large pot. Add water to the pot so that there is a 2-inch (5-cm) layer of water covering the beef. Bring to a boil, skim the foam and immediately remove the beef to a bowl with a slotted spoon. Rinse the pot. Add 5 cups (1.2 L) of hot water to the pot you used to boil the beef and then add the boiled beef, soy sauce, salt, cooking wine, green onions, star anise and the bay leaf and bring to a boil.

While the water is boiling, heat the canola oil in a wok over high heat and then add the dou ban, crushed ginger and Sichuan peppercorns. Stir-fry for about a minute and turn off the heat. After the beef has been boiling for about 10 minutes, add the spice mixture, turn down the heat to low and simmer for 2 hours with the lid on. About 20 minutes before the end of the cooking time, add the radish. Turn up the heat to bring the stew back to a boil and then turn down the heat again and simmer for another 20 minutes. Serve with cilantro and rice.

SESAME SPINACH ROLLS

Zhi Ma Bo Cai Juan

芝麻菠菜卷

YIELDS 2 SERVINGS

INGREDIENTS

8 cups (340 g) fresh spinach

1 tbsp (9 g) white sesame seeds

1–2 tbsp (15–30 ml) Chinese vinegar

1 tbsp (15 ml) sesame oil

1 tbsp (15 ml) soy sauce

1 tsp sugar

Salt, to taste

½ tsp chopped ginger

This is an easy-to-make vegan dish in which the spinach is blanched and rolled into a sushi-style roll, but without rice. It is served with a nutty sesame-flavored dressing. Use young spinach so that you do not wind up with tough stems in the roll.

INSTRUCTIONS

Blanch the spinach in a large pot of boiling water for 10 seconds, then remove and cool in a bowl of ice. Drain the remaining ice and water. Squeeze as much water out of the spinach as you are able.

Place the cooked spinach on a sushi mat and roll it into a long sushi-style roll. If you do not have such a mat, lay the spinach in the center of a large piece of plastic wrap and roll up the sides, forming the spinach into a roll. Cut the roll into six pieces, with each piece being about 1½ to 2 inches (4 to 5 cm) long. Lay the sesame seeds on a small flat serving plate. Dip each end of the spinach pieces in the sesame seeds to coat and place the coated pieces on a serving platter.

In a small bowl, mix the vinegar, sesame oil, soy sauce, sugar, salt and ginger. Serve as a cold dish with the dipping sauce.

TEA EGGS

Cha Ye Dan 茶叶蛋

Tea eggs are a street food in Sichuan but are also made at home. They are eaten for breakfast as well as a snack. The eggs have a marbled appearance after soaking and cooking in a highly fragrant, savory sauce consisting of star anise, cinnamon, Sichuan peppercorns and black tea. I make a dozen at a time and keep them in the refrigerator for up to a week, if they last that long.

YIELDS 12 EGGS

INGREDIENTS

12 large eggs

3 cups (720 ml) water

½ cup (120 ml) soy sauce

2–3 cinnamon sticks

1 tsp Sichuan peppercorns

3–4 star anise

2 tsp (10 g) rock sugar

1¼ tsp (7 g) salt

3½ tsp (7 g) loose black tea

INSTRUCTIONS

Put the eggs in a pot, add enough cold water to cover them by 2 inches (5 cm) and bring the water to a boil. Boil for 7 minutes, then remove the eggs and set aside.

In a clean pot, add the water, soy sauce, cinnamon sticks, Sichuan peppercorns, star anise, rock sugar, salt and the tea. Crack the shell of each egg in several places with the back of a spoon. Handle the eggs carefully and just crack them enough to let the marinade in without breaking the eggs apart. Add the cracked eggs to the pot and bring the liquid to a boil. Then turn the heat to low and simmer for 30 minutes. To get an even better flavor, let the eggs soak in the sauce overnight. Refrigerate unused eggs in the sauce to enjoy later.

SICHUAN CHILI OIL

Shu You La Jiao 熟油辣椒

AND SICHUAN PEPPER-CORN OIL

Hua Jiao You 花椒油

YIELDS 1½ CUPS
(360 ML) OIL

INGREDIENTS

SICHUAN CHILI OIL

1⅓ cups (180 g) ground Sichuan chili powder

1½ cups (360 ml) canola oil

YIELDS ⅓ CUP (80 ML) OIL

INGREDIENTS

SICHUAN PEPPERCORN OIL

⅓ cup (32 g) Sichuan peppercorn powder

⅓ cup (80 ml) canola oil

This simple two-ingredient recipe is an everyday chili oil and Sichuan peppercorn oil. I always have it handy in the pantry. If you start adding too many additional ingredients, it is a chili sauce, not a chili oil. In Sichuan this two-ingredient chili oil is what every family uses at home. Other ingredients such as star anise, garlic and scallions are added while cooking the dish; they are not added into the chili oil jar. Avoid using any oils that have a low smoking point or have a distinct flavor. Canola oil is perfect for making this oil; it doesn't have a strong flavor and has a high smoking point.

INSTRUCTIONS

Put the chili powder in a heatproof Mason jar and the Sichuan peppercorn powder in another jar. Heat the oil to 400°F (200°C), then let it cool down to around 325 to 340°F (160 to 170°C). If the oil is too hot, it will burn the pepper powders.

Pour the hot oil slowly and carefully into the jars until one-third full. Stir to mix, then repeat with a second third, then the last third. After each addition, mix the oil with chopsticks. The oil will sizzle from the heat and give off an amazing aroma. After the jars cool down, screw on the lids and store them at room temperature for up to 3 months. Each time you use the oils, use a clean spoon to remove the oil or powder that settles on the bottom of the jar.

CHAPTER 5
PRESERVED FOODS

Fermented Black Beans, *Dou Chi* 豆豉

Fermented black beans are a very popular Chinese ingredient and are made in many regions of China. Each region makes its own variety, with its own texture and taste. Cantonese *dou chi* are made with small dry beans preserved only in salt. Sichuan fermented black beans are soaked and steamed, allowed to become moldy and then are mixed with salt, liquor and spices. They are fermented for several months and the final flavor of the beans tastes similar to soy sauce. The fermented beans will keep indefinitely. A jar was discovered in *Ma Wang Dui* tomb, the tomb of a high-ranking woman in Hunan Province dated to around 206 B.C. The beans were sealed in a jar that looked the same as the ones you can find today at an Asian market. I use Sichuan black beans in most of my dishes. The famous *Pi Xian dou ban* (fermented broad bean paste) brand **Juan Chen** also makes very good dou chi.

Preserved Vegetable, *Ya Cai* 芽菜

Ya cai is a pickled vegetable made from the stems of mustard greens that grow in southeastern Sichuan Province. Only the plant stems are used. They are dried, mixed with salt and fermented for around 6 months. Then they are mixed with brown sugar and spices and packed in ceramic jars to ferment for a year. The color of ya cai is dark brown and almost looks black. Ya cai is sold two ways: in whole long stems, which you need to wash and cut up yourself in order to use, or already minced in the package. The minced version is called *suimi ya cai*. The best suimi ya cai is made in a town in southeast Sichuan called Yi Bin. In the market, look for brands of suimi ya cai made in Yi Bin.

Pickled Mustard Greens, *Suan Cai* 酸菜

This leafy mustard green with yellow and green leaves is pickled in a salty spiced brine and is sold in packages. You can also buy fresh mustard greens and make *suan cai* at home using my pickle recipe. This pickled vegetable is usually cooked in a soup or stir-fried and pairs well with fish dishes.

Preserved Mustard Stems, *Zha Cai* 榨菜

Zha cai is a type of Sichuan mustard plant stem that differs from the one used to make ya cai and is also called *"da tou cai,"* which translates to "big-headed vegetable." It has a crisp texture and a salty-sour taste. I used to buy them as an afterschool snack from a street food stand. They sold the pickles in slices for one cent apiece. Now I use them in soup, stir-fried noodles, fried rice and many other dishes. They are sold in small packages, which are easy to take on a trip.

Fermented Tofu, *Dou Fu Ru* 豆腐乳

Traditional Chinese cooking is dairy free, so fermented tofu is sometimes seen as the Chinese equivalent of cheese. I use it in cooking but also serve it as a side dish with congee. There are many variations of this tofu, but the two main types are "red" and "white" fermented tofu. In Sichuan, the tofu is fermented with chili oil and spices. The red variety is used more often in cooking than the white one because red fermented tofu is used in dipping sauces, braised dishes and marinades. **Wang Zhi He** is a very famous brand in China. The Chinese province of Taiwanese brand **Jiang Ji** 江记 is one of my favorites, but the label is in Chinese except for one small line that says "sweet alcoholic bean curd."

Fermented Glutinous Rice, *Lao Zao* 醪糟

My grandma used to make *lao zao* at home, so we always had a jar in the house. One of my typical breakfasts growing up was a poached egg in fermented rice. Grains of glutinous rice are suspended in a clear alcoholic liquid (1 to 3% alcohol). It has a sweet rice flavor, so it is also called "sweet rice wine." **Mi Po Po** is one of the popular brands I buy from my local market.

Preserved
Vegetable

Fermented
Tofu

Fermented
Black Beans

Pickled
Mustard Greens

Preserved
Mustard Stems

YA CAI SPRING ROLLS

You Zha Ya Cai Chun Juan
油炸芽菜春卷

When I grew up in Sichuan, spring rolls were only eaten during the Chinese Spring Festival, which is the Chinese New Year. Spring rolls are not usually fried in Sichuan. The wrapper dough is cooked on a grill like a pancake and the spring roll is dipped in a spicy horseradish sauce. But these special spring rolls are fried, with a cooked pork filling. The slightly sweet and salty preserved vegetable, ya cai, gives the dish an umami flavor. Ya cai is also used in dry fried string beans, Dan Dan Noodles (page 75) and bun fillings (page 79).

YIELDS 25 SPRING ROLLS

INGREDIENTS

3 tbsp (45 ml) cooking oil

1 tbsp (6 g) ginger, chopped

1 lb (454 g) ground pork

1 tbsp (15 ml) Chinese cooking wine

4 green onions, chopped

1 tbsp (15 ml) soy sauce

3 tbsp (45 g) preserved vegetable (ya cai)

¾ cup (80 g) carrots, chopped

1 cup (150 g) fresh bamboo, chopped

1 cup (230 g) bean sprouts

1 package spring roll wrappers (25 pieces)

2 tsp (5 g) cornstarch mixed with 3 tbsp (45 ml) water

4 cups (1 L) canola oil, for frying

INSTRUCTIONS

Set the wok over high heat, add the cooking oil and then stir-fry the ginger. Add the ground pork and stir-fry for 2 minutes, then add the cooking wine and continue to stir-fry until the pork is opaque, 1 to 2 minutes. Add the green onions, season with soy sauce and then add the ya cai. Mix well with the meat and stir-fry for another couple of minutes. Mix in the carrots and bamboo and then add the bean sprouts. Stir-fry for another 10 seconds. Remove the filling from the wok, place in a bowl and set aside to cool. The filling can be used right away, but it is easier to use it after cooling down in the refrigerator for 30 minutes.

Lay a spring roll wrapper diagonally on a flat surface so one corner is pointing towards you. Take 2 to 3 tablespoons (30 to 45 g) of filling and place it 2 to 3 inches (5 to 7.5 cm) from the corner closest to you. Roll the corner over the filling and press down on each side of the filling to flatten the wrapper. Fold the left and right sides of the wrapper towards the middle. Stir the cornstarch slurry and, with your finger, brush it onto the corner of the wrapper opposite the filling. Roll the wrapper into a tight seal. Place the sealed side down on a sheet pan or cutting board lined with parchment paper. Heat a pot of canola oil to 320°F (160°C) and deep-fry a few spring rolls at a time for about 3 minutes, turning every minute to ensure that all the sides are golden brown. When done, place on a plate lined with a paper towel to absorb the oil and serve.

CHINESE BARBECUED PORK

Char Siu, Mi Zhi Cha Shao
蜜汁叉烧肉

This is an all-purpose Cantonese barbecued pork recipe. You can slice it and eat it or use it in other dishes such as fried rice or fried noodles. I use it to make the filling for steamed pork buns, *cha shao bao (char siu bao)*. The pork can be cooked in the oven, but it gets its name from the fork (*char*) used to hold it over a charcoal grill. The red bean curd that is used in many of my recipes is used here as a flavor enhancer in the pork marinade. The red tofu cubes are usually mashed prior to adding to the marinade.

YIELDS 6 TO 8 SERVINGS

INGREDIENTS

PORK MARINADE

3 tbsp (45 ml) soy sauce

1 tbsp (15 ml) oyster sauce

3 tbsp (45 g) sugar

2 tbsp (30 ml) Shaoxing cooking wine

2 pieces fermented red tofu

1 tbsp (15 ml) liquid from fermented red tofu

1 tsp five spice powder

1 tbsp (15 g) chopped garlic

3 lb (1.4 kg) pork shoulder

FOR BASTING

2 tbsp (30 ml) honey

1 tbsp (15 ml) water

Rice, for serving

INSTRUCTIONS

To make the marinade, mix the soy sauce, oyster sauce, sugar, cooking wine, fermented red tofu and 1 tablespoon (15 ml) of the liquid from the tofu, five spice powder and chopped garlic in a large bowl. Cut the pork shoulder into five or six pieces and marinate the pork in the sauce overnight or for at least 3 hours in the refrigerator.

Remove the pork from the refrigerator and let it adjust to room temperature for 30 minutes. Meanwhile, preheat the oven to 400°F (200°C). Mix the honey and water in a small bowl. Place the pork pieces on a pan and place in the oven. Cook for 15 minutes and then brush the pork with the honey and water mixture. Cook for another 15 minutes, then turn over the pork slices and brush on more of the honey and water mixture. Continue to cook for another 15 minutes or until the internal temperature of the pork reaches 145°F (63°C). Slice the pork and serve hot with rice.

GOLDEN FRIED RICE

WITH PRESERVED MUSTARD STEMS

Huang Jin Zha Cai Chao Fan 黄金榨菜炒饭

YIELDS 4 SERVINGS

INGREDIENTS

2 cups + 7 tbsp (454 g) leftover rice

3 egg yolks

2 tbsp (30 ml) cooking oil

1 green onion, chopped, divided

2 Chinese sausages, chopped

1 tbsp (12 g) lard

¼ cup (60 g) chopped zha cai

Salt, to taste

This Cantonese rice dish is over 1,500 years old. The rice is coated in egg yolk before stir-frying, which results in the fried rice resembling flakes of gold. I mix the rice and egg by hand to get a very even coating. There are many versions of this dish—some use seafood, but mine uses Chinese sausage and *zha cai.* Zha cai adds a savory flavor and crunchy texture to the rice.

INSTRUCTIONS

Put the rice in a large bowl and add the egg yolks. Mix the rice and yolks by hand until the rice is completely coated with the yolks. Heat the wok over medium-high heat and add the cooking oil.

When the oil is hot, add half of the chopped green onion and the sausages and stir-fry until fragrant. Add the rice and stir-fry for about 2 minutes. Add the lard and zha cai and mix well. Add salt to taste. When the rice bounces off the sides of the wok, it is ready. Mix in the remaining green onion and serve hot.

STIR-FRIED CHICKEN WITH PRESERVED VEGETABLE

Ji Mi Ya Cai 鸡米芽菜

YIELDS 4 SERVINGS

INGREDIENTS

1 tsp salt

1 tsp cornstarch

1 tbsp (15 ml) cooking wine

¾ lb (340 g) minced chicken breast

3 tbsp (45 ml) cooking oil

2 tsp (10 g) chopped garlic

5 tsp (10 g) chopped ginger

3 tbsp (15 g) red chilis, chopped (optional)

10 tbsp (150 g) preserved Chinese mustard greens (ya cai)

1 tbsp (6 g) chopped green onion

This is a versatile Sichuan dish that can be served as a main course, used as a noodle dish topping or eaten inside steamed bread as a sandwich. The *ya cai* gives the chicken an umami flavor. Traditionally, chicken breast is used, but you can substitute with chicken thigh, pork or even beef. For a vegan version, try using shiitake mushrooms.

INSTRUCTIONS

Begin with making the marinade by combining the salt, cornstarch and cooking wine in a medium-sized bowl and add the chicken breast. Marinate for 15 minutes.

Heat the cooking oil in the wok over high heat, add the marinated chicken and stir-fry until the chicken turns opaque and a little dry, about 3 minutes. Move the chicken to a clean bowl and set aside. Put the garlic, ginger and chilis in the wok, stir-fry for a minute over high heat, then add the ya cai. Continue to stir-fry for about 30 seconds to release the fragrance from the ya cai. Return the chicken to the wok and stir-fry until all the ingredients are well mixed. Add the green onion, toss with the chicken and serve hot.

FISH
WITH FERMENTED BLACK BEANS

Dou Chi Yu Tiao 豆豉鱼条

YIELDS 4 SERVINGS

INGREDIENTS

1 lb (454 g) white fish filets, such as tilapia or haddock

¼ tsp salt

5 tsp (10 g) ginger, sliced

3 green onions, cut into 2-inch (5-cm) pieces, divided

3 tbsp (45 ml) Shaoxing cooking wine, divided

¼ cup (60 ml) cooking oil

1¾ oz (50 g) ground pork

2 tbsp (40 g) fermented black beans (dou chi)

5 tsp (10 g) ginger, crushed

½ cup (120 ml) chicken stock or hot water

1 tbsp (15 ml) soy sauce

1 tsp sugar

1 tbsp (15 ml) sesame oil

This is a very traditional but nonspicy Sichuan fish dish. I panfry the fish in a wok, but originally the fish was deep-fried. It is served as a main course and is often served with bai jiu, Chinese liquor. *Dou chi*, fermented black beans, are an intensely savory flavor enhancer that develop a more complex flavor when cooked in oil. Combining the beans with soy sauce and cooking wine adds layers of flavor to the fish. This sauce also brings a delicious flavor to vegetables like broccoli, cauliflower and string beans. For a vegan version, use dried shiitake mushroom instead of the ground pork.

INSTRUCTIONS

Cut the fish into 4 x 1-inch (10 x 2.5-cm) strips and marinate with the marinade made from salt, sliced ginger, pieces of 1 green onion and 2 tablespoons (30 ml) of cooking wine in a medium-sized bowl for 20 minutes.

Heat the cooking oil in a wok over high heat and fry the fish until golden brown, about 2 minutes. Remove the fish with a slotted spoon and set aside on a plate lined with a paper towel to absorb excess oil. Leave about 2 tablespoons (30 ml) of oil in the wok and discard the rest. Heat the oil over high heat, add the ground pork and stir-fry for 2 minutes or until the pork is opaque. Add the fermented black beans, ginger and pieces of 2 green onions and stir-fry with the pork until fragrant.

Return the fish to the wok and carefully mix everything together so as not to break the fish. Add the stock, soy sauce, sugar and the remaining cooking wine. Cook for a few more minutes over medium-high heat until the liquid is boiling. Drizzle the sesame oil on top and serve.

POACHED EGGS IN SWEET FERMENTED RICE

Hong Tang Lao Zao Dan
红糖醪糟蛋

YIELDS 1 SERVING

INGREDIENTS

2 cups (480 ml) warm water

2 tsp (14 g) molasses or brown sugar

6 goji berries

1½ cups (113 g) rice cakes

1⅓ tbsp (20 g) fermented glutinous rice

2 eggs

This is a common breakfast in China and I still eat it frequently. The sweet taste of fermented rice complements the richness of the bright creamy egg yolk. This breakfast makes you feel warm, energetic and ready for a new day! In the first month after giving birth in China, women traditionally stay home in bed and eat this dish since it is considered an excellent way for them to regain their strength.

INSTRUCTIONS

Pour the water into a medium pot, add the molasses and goji berries and bring to a boil. Add the rice cakes and continue to cook until they are floating at the top of the water, about 5 minutes. Turn the heat down to low, add the fermented rice and stir. Crack the eggs into the pot, but do not stir. Cook the eggs for 1 minute over low heat, then turn off the heat and cover for 3 minutes. Transfer to a bowl and serve hot.

STIR-FRIED SOYBEANS

WITH PICKLED VEGETABLE

Qin Dou Chao Suan Cai
青豆炒酸菜

YIELDS 4 SERVINGS

INGREDIENTS

2 tbsp (30 ml) cooking oil

3½ tsp (7 g) ginger, peeled and sliced

2 small fresh red chili peppers, chopped

15 tbsp (225 g) pickled mustard greens (suan cai), chopped into small pieces

2⅔ cups (453 g) green soybeans (edamame)

Salt, to taste

These days you can buy soybeans in almost any market in the frozen vegetable section. They are sold both in and out of the shell and I prefer to buy them shelled. The soybeans are stir-fried with *suan cai* and the dish is served as a vegetable entree. You may substitute almost any bean, even a canned bean, for the soybeans. The pickled mustard greens release salty and sour flavors and a powerful fragrance.

INSTRUCTIONS

Heat the wok over high heat, add the cooking oil and when hot, add the ginger and chili peppers. Stir-fry until they release their fragrance. Add the pickled mustard greens, stir-fry for 1 minute and then add the soybeans. Continue to stir-fry for 3 minutes, then add some salt to taste and serve with dinner or lunch.

ZHA CAI
PORK EGG DROP SOUP

Zha Cai Rou Si Tang
榨菜肉丝汤

YIELDS 4 SERVINGS

INGREDIENTS

2 tbsp (30 ml) cooking oil

2½ tbsp (15 g) ginger, chopped into slivers

2 tbsp (12 g) green onion, finely chopped, plus more for optional garnish

5 tbsp + 1 tsp (80 g) preserved mustard stems (zha cai)

8 oz (225 g) pork tenderloin, cut into slivers

6 cups (1.4 L) gao tang (page 40) or hot water

3¼ cups (225 g) bok choy

2 eggs

1 tbsp (15 ml) water

1 tsp cornstarch

Pinch of white pepper powder

This is the Sichuan version of egg drop soup. The sour flavor comes from the *zha cai*, not vinegar. Soup is part of a typical shared family meal cooked at home, **san cai yi tang** (three dishes, one soup). The meal consists of one soup dish, one vegetable dish and two more dishes, usually one meat and one seafood dish.

INSTRUCTIONS

Place the oil in a medium-sized pot over high heat. When the oil is hot, add the ginger and green onion and stir-fry until fragrant, for about 1 minute. Add the zha cai and stir-fry a few more times. Add the pork and stir-fry over high heat for about 2 minutes or until it turns opaque. Add the gao tang to the pot, bring to a boil and then turn the heat to medium-low. Drop in the bok choy.

In a mixing bowl, mix the eggs, water and cornstarch with a whisk. Whisk until everything is well blended. Use a spatula to stir the soup clockwise and then gradually drizzle in the egg mixture while continuing to stir the soup in a clockwise direction. The egg mixture will turn into little ribbons. Remove the pot from the heat. Add the white pepper and garnish with extra green onion, if desired.

HOMEMADE
SICHUAN
PICKLES

Sichuan Pao Cai 四川泡菜

YIELDS 10 SERVINGS

INGREDIENTS

1 quart (1 L) filtered water

3 tbsp + ½ tsp (57 g) salt

1½ cups (225 g) red radishes or daikon radishes, skin on

4 oz (113 g) celery

4 oz (113 g) round cabbage

4 oz (113 g) broccoli stems

1 tbsp (14 g) rock sugar or brown sugar

2 tbsp (30 ml) bai jiu (Chinese liquor) or vodka

5 tsp (10 g) dried Sichuan peppercorns

4½ tsp (14 g) fresh long red chili peppers or dried Sichuan chili peppers

1½ cups + 1 tbsp (150 g) ginger, peeled and cut into large pieces

2 tbsp (30 g) garlic, peeled

I use a traditional Sichuan pickle jar with a lid and a water seal. This way, you can keep the original brine indefinitely. The pickle jars are made of glass or clay. Make sure the water seal doesn't dry out. Keep adding water around the top every few days. To maintain a good brine, add more salt, sugar and liquor every time you add fresh vegetables. Sometimes a white film may form on top. This white growth is not mold. It is *kahm* yeast, which is a natural byproduct of lacto-fermentation. If you see this on top of your brine, skim it off with a sterile spoon and add a little liquor and garlic.

I use plastic wrap to cover the jar when I am on vacation so the water seal won't dry out. This method will keep the pickle jar water seal good for 7 to 10 days. If I am away from home longer than 10 days, I carefully dry out the water seal. ONLY add vegetable oil around the jar, instead of the water, because oil won't dry out. Make sure the oil won't get into the jar. Carefully clean out the oil seal when you come back from vacation and add the water seal like before.

INSTRUCTIONS

Wash and sterilize a Chinese pickle jar and its lid in boiling water. Bring the filtered water to a boil and then turn off the heat. Add the salt and stir to dissolve. Set aside and let cool to room temperature.

Rinse the vegetables and keep the red radishes whole with the skin. If you use daikon radishes, cut them into bite-sized pieces. Remove any strings from the celery and cut it into 5- to 6-inch (13- to 15-cm) pieces. Cut the round cabbage into quarters or smaller pieces that fit in your jar. Peel the broccoli stems and cut them into long pieces. Let the vegetables dry completely. Add the salt water to the jar. It should reach about halfway up your jar. Add the rock sugar, bai jiu, Sichuan peppercorns, red chilis, ginger and garlic. Add the vegetables, leaving an inch or two (2.5 or 5 cm) of empty space at the top of the jar. Put the lid on the jar and add water around the air lock. The first batch of pickles takes a couple of weeks to ferment. Open the lid for a few seconds during the first week to let the gas out. When the vegetables are pickled, you should smell a sour, fragrant aroma when you open the jar.

Once your pickle jar is established, fresh vegetables will only take 1 to 3 days to pickle. The flavor of the pickles will continue to improve with each batch and it may take at least 3 months for an optimal flavor.

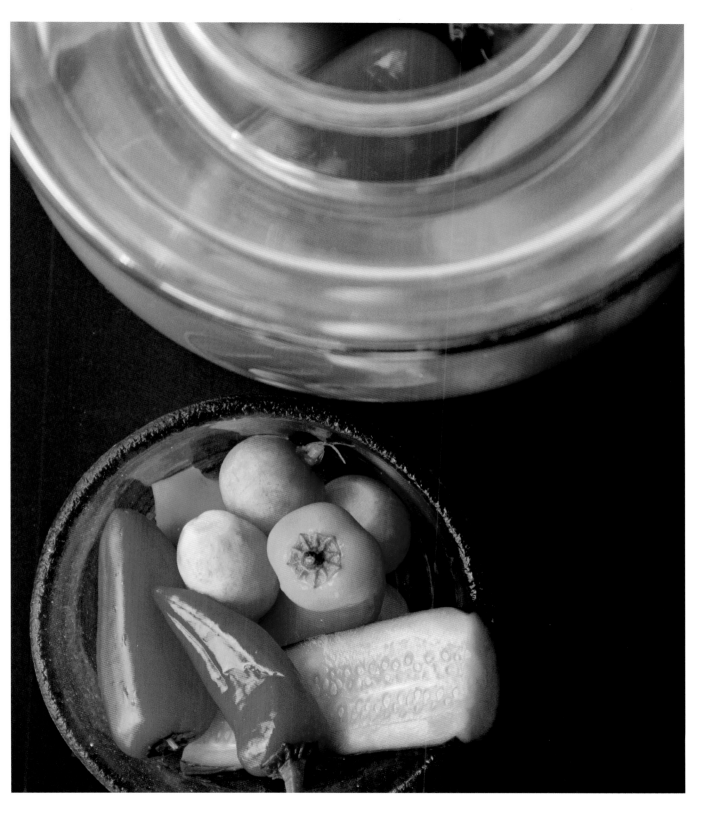

SWEETS

Tea, *Cha* 茶

After water, tea is the most widely consumed drink in the world. In China, people drink tea all day long. There are seven types of tea in China: green tea, blue tea (oolong tea), white tea, yellow tea, black tea, dark tea and *Pu erh* tea. A lot of the tea you will see at an Asian market is of low quality, but here are some high-quality teas you can find there as well.

The good-quality teas are sold as loose tea leaves in a container. Some examples are:

GREEN TEA
Dragon Well, *Long Jing* 龙井
Green Snail Spring, *Bi Lou Chun* 碧螺春
Jasmine Green Tea, *Mo Li Hua Cha* 茉莉花茶
Emei Zhu Ye Qing 峨眉竹叶青

OOLONG TEA
Iron Goddess, *Tie Guan Yin* 铁观音
Dong Ding Oolong 冻顶乌龙
High Mountain *Oolong* 高山乌龙
Da Hong Pao Oolong 大红袍

BLACK TEA
Yu Nan Dian Hong 云南滇红
Jin Jun Mei Black Tea 金骏眉
Lapsang Souchong Black Tea, *Zheng San Xiao Zhong* 正三小种

Tapioca Flour, *Mu Shu Feng* 木薯粉

Tapioca flour is also called tapioca starch. It is gluten free, slightly sweet and great for gluten-free baking. It is also used as a thickening agent in soups, sauces and pie fillings.

The common brands you can find are **ERAWAN** tapioca starch and **Bob's Red Mill** tapioca flour.

Agar-Agar Powder, *Qiong Zhi* 琼脂

Agar-agar powder is made from seaweed and contains no animal product. It is a great substitute for gelatin egg whites. Replace one egg white with 1 tablespoon (2 g) of agar-agar powder mixed with 1 tablespoon (15 ml) of water. Whisk and chill in the refrigerator. Once the mixture has cooled, take it out of the refrigerator and whisk it a second time. It is now ready to use as an egg white substitute in your recipe.

Mung Beans, *Lu Dou* 绿豆

Mung beans are called *lu dou*, which means green beans in Chinese. They are used in both savory and sweet dishes. Dried mung beans can often be found in packages in the aisle with other beans and grains.

Red Beans, *Hong Dou* 红豆

Red beans are sometimes called adzuki or azuki. Originating from China, they are popular in Asian cooking. Red beans are used in many sweet dessert dishes, such as Red Bean Paste (page 153), sweet red bean soup and red bean cakes.

Tremella Mushroom, *Yin Er* 银耳

Tremella, or silver ear mushroom, is a gourmet and medicinal mushroom. It is commonly used in medicinal soup for nourishing the body, curing a cough and clearing heat in the lungs. It is also considered the ultimate anti-aging mushroom.

Glutinous
Rice Flour

Red Beans

Mung Beans

Tapioca Starch

Agar-Agar
Powder

MOON CAKES

Yue Bing 月饼

YIELDS 2 DOZEN (1.8-OZ
[50-G]) MOON CAKES

INGREDIENTS

GOLDEN SYRUP

6 cups (1.2 kg) granulated sugar

1 quart (1 L) water

Juice of 1 lime

1 tbsp (1 g) maltose or malt sugar

MOON CAKES

13 tbsp + 1 tsp (200 ml) golden syrup, homemade or store-bought

2¼ tsp (11 ml) alkaline water *(kan sui)*

¼ tsp baking soda

4 tbsp (60 ml) corn oil

½ tsp molasses, for coloring

2 cups (250 g) all-purpose flour, plus more for dusting

Red Bean Paste (page 153) or Black Sesame Paste (page 154)

1 egg yolk + 2 tsp (10 ml) water, for egg wash

Every year in China we eat moon cakes for the Mid-Autumn Festival 中秋节, also known as the Moon festival. This is the most important Chinese holiday after the Chinese New Year. Moon cakes are rich pastries typically filled with sweet bean or lotus seed paste. The combination of Red Bean Paste (page 153) and the outer skin gives this variety of moon cake a smooth texture and rich flavor, making it a very popular moon cake flavor. The white lotus paste, which is made from fresh lotus seeds, has a natural fragrance. The Mid-Autumn Festival is a time for friends and family to come together. I am now living in the United States, far from my family and friends in China, and eating moon cakes reminds me of past holidays spent with them.

INSTRUCTIONS

Add all of the syrup ingredients except the maltose to a pot over high heat and cook until the sugar has dissolved. Turn down the heat and simmer until the syrup turns a light golden color. Turn off the heat, add the maltose and stir until dissolved. Let cool and then put the syrup in a clean jar. Close the lid and store in a cool, dry area. The syrup can be prepared months in advance. It is better to let the syrup mature, as this will produce a better moon cake dough and improve the shelf life of the moon cakes.

In a bowl, mix the golden syrup, alkaline water, baking soda and corn oil. Mix well and set the mixture aside for 15 minutes. Add the molasses to the syrup mixture, mix well, then gradually add the flour. Mix together to form a smooth, soft dough. Cover the dough with plastic wrap and let rest for 3 hours. Transfer the dough to a floured surface and divide it into 0.7-ounce (20-g) balls. Divide the Red Bean Paste into 1-ounce (30-g) balls. Sprinkle some flour on one moon cake dough ball and roll it into the shape of a round dumpling wrapper. Place one filling ball in the center of the dough and seal the edges of the dough around the filling. Ensure that the dough is completely sealed. Dust one 1.8-oz (50-g) moon cake mold with flour and shake out any excess flour. Press the ball of dough into the mold, then lightly tap out the moon cake.

(continued)

Place the moon cakes on a baking sheet lined with a silicone baking mat or on a greased baking tray. Spray some water on the top of each moon cake. Bake at 390°F (200°C) for 5 minutes. Then, remove the moon cakes from the oven and let them cool for a few minutes. Lightly brush the egg wash onto each moon cake. If you use too much egg wash, the pattern on the top of the moon cake will not show very well. Bake the moon cakes at 355°F (180°C) for 15 minutes, until golden. Freshly baked moon cakes are crispy on the outside. Store them at room temperature in a partially closed container for 2 or 3 days so that the dough softens and is no longer crispy. At this point, they are ready to eat.

VEGAN AGAR-AGAR JELLY FRUIT CAKE

Shui Guo Yan Cai Guo Dong Dan Gao
水果燕菜果冻蛋糕

YIELDS 4 TO 6 SERVINGS

INGREDIENTS

FRUIT LAYER

2 cups (475 g) chopped pieces fruit of your choice, such as oranges, blueberries, mango, dragon fruit and strawberries

2 tsp (1 g) agar-agar powder

2 cups (480 ml) water

¼ cup (50 g) sugar

COCONUT MILK LAYER

⅔ cup (160 ml) coconut milk

⅓ cup (80 ml) water

1 tsp agar-agar powder

3 tbsp (45 g) sugar

This cake consists of three layers of agar-agar. The bottom layer is agar-agar and fruit juice. The middle layer is agar-agar and coconut milk and the top layer is agar-agar with pieces of cut-up fruit. Choose whatever fruit you like and make a decorative arrangement in the pan. This light gelatinous fruity dessert is a showstopper for summer parties and is also gluten free and vegan!

INSTRUCTIONS

Cut the fruit into small cubes and set aside. Add the agar-agar powder and water to a saucepan and whisk until mixed. Turn on the heat and continue to stir until it comes to a boil. Boil for 40 seconds to a minute, until the agar-agar dissolves. Test with a spoon to see if any specks of agar-agar powder stick to the spoon. If there are no specks, that means all the powder has dissolved and you can move on to the next step. Add the sugar to the saucepan, mix until dissolved and then remove the pan from the heat. Immediately pour some of the agar-agar mixture into an 8-inch (20-cm) round cake pan or mold so that it makes a ¼-inch (6-mm)-thick layer. Arrange the fruit pieces in the mixture, making an attractive pattern. Next, pour the rest of the agar-agar mixture slowly over the fruit. Let the mixture set at room temperature for a few minutes or until the surface is firm enough to pour on the second layer.

Make the coconut milk layer while waiting for the fruit layer to set. Add the coconut milk, water and agar-agar powder to a saucepan and whisk to dissolve. Turn on the heat and keep whisking constantly. Once the mixture comes to a boil, let it cook for 40 seconds to a minute, or until everything has dissolved. Then, add the sugar and mix again until dissolved and turn off the heat.

Check the first layer by touching it gently with your finger. If the top layer has set, slowly pour the hot coconut milk mixture on top of it. Allow it to sit at room temperature and it will set in about 10 minutes.

(continued)

JUICE LAYER

¼ cup (60 ml) water

1 tsp agar-agar powder

¾ cup (180 ml) fruit juice of your choice, such as orange, mango or pineapple juice

1 tsp sugar (optional)

Using the same method, make the juice layer. Add the water, agar-agar powder and juice to a saucepan and bring to a boil. Then, add the sugar (if using). If you use an acidic juice such as orange juice, make sure you do not boil the juice any longer than necessary because it will break down the agar-agar and the layer will not set.

Pour the hot juice mixture over the coconut milk layer and put the cake in the refrigerator for 2 hours. To remove the cake from the pan, use an offset spatula to loosen the cake from the edges of the pan. Place four evenly spaced toothpicks between the cake and the edge of the pan to create some space between the two. Place a large plate over the cake mold and flip the cake mold over. Gently tap the bottom of the pan to release the cake. The fruit layer will now be on top. Cut the cake into slices and serve on a plate.

BOBA TAPIOCA PEARLS

Bo Ba Zhen Zhu 波霸珍珠

YIELDS 4 SERVINGS

INGREDIENTS

1¾ cups (420 ml) water, divided

4½ tbsp (90 g) molasses, divided

½ cup (100 g) tapioca flour, divided, plus 2 tbsp (25 g) for rolling the dough

These boba pearls are chewy and gelatinous. They are an important component of bubble milk tea drinks that are originally from the Chinese province of Taiwan but are now common everywhere. They are naturally gluten free!

INSTRUCTIONS

Add ¼ cup (60 ml) of water and 4 tablespoons (80 g) of molasses to a pot, bring to a boil and then turn the heat down to medium. Add 2 tablespoons (25 g) of the tapioca flour and mix. When combined, add the rest of the flour and mix well to form a dough.

On a flat surface, sprinkle 2 tablespoons (25 g) of tapioca flour, then transfer the dough to the flour on top of the work surface. Knead the dough while it is hot until it is smooth. Divide the dough into three pieces and roll each piece into a long noodle shape. Cut each noodle-shaped piece of dough into pearl-sized pieces. Roll each small piece into a ball.

Boil the remaining 1½ cups (360 ml) of water and ½ tablespoon (10 g) of molasses in a pot and once boiling, add the boba pearls. Cook for about 3 to 4 minutes, then drain the pearls and put them in a bowl of cold water. They are ready to use in any boba tea.

BUBBLE TEA WITH CREAM CHEESE FOAM TOPPING

Hei Tang Zhen Zhu Nai Cha
黑糖珍珠奶茶

YIELDS 1 SERVING

INGREDIENTS

MILK TEA

2 tsp (10 g) sugar

1 cup (240 ml) milk

¼ cup (60 ml) water

2 black tea bags

CREAM CHEESE TOPPING

1 tbsp (15 g) cream cheese

1 tsp sugar

Pinch of salt

¼ cup (60 ml) heavy cream

2 tbsp (14 g) cooked boba pearls (page 146)

The pearls used in boba tea are made from tapioca flour. They have a chewy texture and a flavor similar to licorice and are able to absorb the milk and flavor of the tea. The cream cheese foam topping adds a layer of rich, creamy flavor.

INSTRUCTIONS

In a small pot, melt the sugar and cook until caramelized, then add the milk and water. After everything is combined, add the tea bags and continue to cook for another 10 to 15 minutes over medium heat. Remove the tea bags, then pour the milk tea into a container and set aside.

Make the topping by adding the cream cheese, sugar and salt to a bowl. Using a handheld or stand mixer with the whisk attachment, whisk the ingredients together and then add the heavy cream. Whisk the ingredients into a foamy consistency. Place the boba pearls in a glass, add the milk tea and add a scoop of the foam topping.

HOMEMADE MOCHI

Ma Shu 麻糬

Mochi is a Japanese rice cake made from glutinous rice flour. My kids' favorite filling is Red Bean Paste (page 153), but you can use Black Sesame Paste (page 154), lotus paste or fresh fruits like strawberries and mandarin oranges. The mochi has a sticky, stretchy, soft and chewy texture. The sweet filling pairs perfectly with the chewy texture of the mochi. This is a gluten-free dessert.

YIELDS 10 PIECES

INGREDIENTS

1 cup (110 g) glutinous rice flour, plus 1 tbsp (7 g) for rolling the dough

2 tbsp (16 g) cornstarch

2 tbsp (30 g) sugar

¾ cup (180 ml) milk

1 tbsp (14 g) butter, room temperature

10 tbsp (210 g) Red Bean Paste (page 153)

INSTRUCTIONS

In a mixing bowl, combine the glutinous rice flour, cornstarch and sugar, then slowly add the milk. Whisk until it becomes a smooth batter. Cover the batter with plastic wrap and put in a steamer for 25 to 30 minutes. You can use a microwave if you prefer. Poke a few small holes in the plastic wrap and microwave for 5 to 6 minutes. Remove the bowl from the steamer and add the butter to the hot mochi dough.

Knead the dough until smooth, then wrap the dough and put it in the refrigerator for 1 hour. Roast 1 tablespoon (7 g) of glutinous rice flour in a pan until it turns light brown, then sprinkle the roasted flour on a flat surface. Place the dough on top of the roasted flour and roll it into a log shape. Cut the log into 10 equal pieces. Take each piece, press it down and using a rolling pin, roll it into a ½-inch (1-cm)-thick disc.

Place 1 tablespoon (21 g) of the Red Bean Paste in a wrapper, enclose the filling and seal it on the bottom. Repeat for the remaining pieces. Eat as a snack with afternoon tea or as an after-dinner treat.

RED BEAN
PASTE

Hong Dou Sha 红豆沙

YIELDS 3 CUPS (700 G) PASTE

INGREDIENTS

1¼ cups (250 g) dried red soybeans

2½ cups (600 ml) water

⅜ cup + 2 tsp (100 ml) corn oil

½ cup (100 g) sugar

10 cups (100 g) maltose

I use this red bean paste in several dishes: mochi (page 150), Chinese sweet rice balls and Chinese steamed buns. Store in the refrigerator for up to a week or divide it into small portions and freeze it for up to a few months.

INSTRUCTIONS

Wash the beans, place them in a pressure cooker with the water and cook for 35 minutes. If you do not have a pressure cooker, soak the beans for 1 hour and then cook on the stove for about 1 hour until the beans are soft and easy to mash with a spoon.

Drain the water, put the cooked beans in a blender and blend into a paste. Place the paste in a nonstick pan and cook over low heat, stirring with a spatula for 3 minutes. Add half of the corn oil and continue to stir until the oil is absorbed. Add the rest of the oil and stir until well mixed.

After all the oil has been absorbed, blend in the sugar, followed by the maltose. Continue to stir and cook over low heat for 15 to 20 minutes. Store in an airtight container in the refrigerator.

BLACK
SESAME
PASTE

Hei Zhi Ma Xian 黑芝麻馅

YIELDS ¾ CUP (200 G)
PASTE

INGREDIENTS

13⅓ tbsp (120 g) black sesame
seeds

2 tbsp (30 g) sugar

6⅔ tbsp (80 g) butter or softened
lard

The black sesame paste has a roasted nutty flavor with deep earthy undertones. It is often sweetened with sugar or honey and makes a good filling for steamed buns, Moon Cakes (page 140), Tang Yuan (page 157) and mochi (page 150).

INSTRUCTIONS

Toast the sesame seeds in a pan over low heat, 5 to 6 minutes. After the sesame seeds are cool, put them in a food processor and process with the sugar until you have a paste-like consistency. Mix in the butter and then refrigerate until firm.

SWEET GLUTINOUS RICE BALLS

Tang Yuan 汤圆

YIELDS 20 RICE BALLS,
ABOUT 4 SERVINGS

INGREDIENTS

1 cup + 13 tbsp (200 g) sweet rice flour (glutinous rice flour)

⅔–¾ cup (160–180 ml) hot water

Red Bean Paste (page 153) or Black Sesame Paste (page 154), cold

Tang yuan is a Chinese sweet traditionally eaten on the 15th day of Chinese New Year, also called the "Lantern Festival." In Chinese, tang yuan is a homophone for a family reunion and eating them will ensure a prosperous and lucky New Year. The rice balls can be made with or without filling. This is another gluten-free dessert that I eat for breakfast sometimes!

INSTRUCTIONS

Put the rice flour in a bowl and gradually add ⅔ cup (160 ml) of hot water to mix with the flour. Add additional water as needed until you have a soft, smooth dough. Wrap with plastic wrap or a damp cloth. Divide the Red Bean Paste into 20 (3.5-ounce [10-g]) balls. Divide the dough into 1-ounce (30-g) pieces and roll each one into a ball.

Take one dough ball and press down in the center, making a bowl shape. Place a ball of filling in the center. Gently push the wrapper upwards to completely seal it and then roll it around between your palms to form it into a ball.

Bring a pot of water to a boil and gently slide the tang yuan into the water. Push them around the pot with the back of a spoon to prevent them from sticking to the bottom of the pot. Turn the heat to medium-low and cook for about 5 minutes, until they all float on the surface. Serve in a bowl with some of the cooking liquid.

MUNG BEAN CAKES

Lu Dou Gao 绿豆糕

YIELDS 18 CAKES

INGREDIENTS

1 cup + 10 tbsp (336 g) dried peeled mung beans

10 tbsp (150 ml) corn oil or butter, plus more for greasing

5 tbsp (75 g) corn syrup

9 tbsp (115 g) sugar

1 tsp matcha powder (optional)

These cakes are eaten for a lunar holiday called the Dragon Boat Festival, which occurs on the fifth day of the fifth lunar month. Although they are not moon cakes, they are made with a moon cake mold. The cake is very rich and dense with a mild bean flavor. The optional matcha powder adds another Asian flavor to the cake. They make a great dessert to eat with Chinese tea! Use corn oil for a vegan version.

INSTRUCTIONS

Soak the beans for at least 5 to 6 hours or overnight. Line the bottom of a steamer tray with a large piece of cheesecloth and steam the beans over high heat for 60 minutes. Remove the beans from the steamer to a bowl and mash them into a paste.

Heat a nonstick pan over medium-low heat and add the bean paste and corn oil. Mix with a spatula until all the oil has been absorbed by the beans. Add the corn syrup, sugar and matcha powder (if using) and mix over low heat until the bean mixture can be shaped into a ball. Remove from the heat.

Hold a potato ricer over an empty pot or bowl and add the bean mixture. Squeeze the handles of the ricer together until the bean mixture begins extruding through the holes. If you don't have a ricer, use a mesh sieve and press the beans through with a spatula. Divide the bean paste into 1.75-ounce (50-g) portions and roll each into a ball.

Grease a 1.8-ounce (50-g) mold with corn oil, place one bean paste ball into the mold and press it into a cake. Repeat with the remaining bean paste balls. They are ready to eat right away. Store in the refrigerator for up to 5 days.

RAINDROP
CAKE

Shui Xin Xuan Bing
水信玄饼

YIELDS 2 SERVINGS

INGREDIENTS

1–2 salted cherry blossoms

1¾ cups (420 ml) water

¼ tsp sugar

¼ tsp agar-agar powder

TOPPING

½ tsp roasted soybean powder

1 tbsp (20 g) molasses or honey

This is a Japanese dessert that looks like a raindrop when it comes out of the mold. This cake looks beautiful and is incredibly tasty with a slightly sweet and toasty flavor from soybean powder. It just melts in your mouth. Serve it with molasses or honey on top.

INSTRUCTIONS

Soak the salted cherry blossoms in water for 10 minutes and put aside. Add the 1¾ cups (420 ml) of water to a small pot along with the sugar and agar-agar powder. Mix well and cook over medium-high heat.

After it comes to a boil, cook for 1 minute, stirring with a spatula. Make sure all of the agar-agar powder has dissolved by putting the back of a spoon into the mixture and looking for powder flakes. If you see flakes, continue to cook for 30 seconds and check again. Turn off the heat after no flakes appear.

Place the cherry blossoms in the center of a 3½ x 3½ x 6½–inch (9 x 9 x 16.5–cm) spherical ice mold and add all of the agar-agar mixture. Chill in the refrigerator for 3 hours or overnight. Serve within 20 minutes of removing the cake from the mold. Top with the soybean powder and drizzle molasses or honey over it.

SILVER EAR
MUSHROOM SOUP

Yin Er Tang 银耳汤

This sweet soup is not served as a dessert in China. It is eaten as a breakfast or snack to improve your health. The mushrooms, pear and goji berries are considered medicinal. People eat it to ward off coughs and colds as well as to improve their complexion. Chinese herbs are often added, but my version just has the mushrooms, pear and goji berries. Make sure to cut up the mushrooms so that when cooked thoroughly, the soup will have a velvety texture.

YIELDS 4 TO 6 SERVINGS

INGREDIENTS

1 large head silver ear mushrooms or 2–3 smaller heads

1 tbsp (10 g) goji berries

6 cups (1.4 L) water

1 Asian pear, cut into cubes

4 tbsp (60 g) rock sugar, or to taste

INSTRUCTIONS

Soak the silver ear mushrooms in warm water for 30 minutes and then using scissors or your hands, break them into smaller pieces. Soak the goji berries in a small bowl with cold water and set aside.

Add 6 cups (1.4 L) of water to a pot and bring to a boil. When the water boils, add the silver ear mushrooms and pear. Simmer for 45 minutes, then add the goji berries and rock sugar. Simmer for another 15 minutes and serve hot.

ACKNOWLEDGMENTS

Writing this book was harder than I thought and more rewarding than I could have ever imagined. None of this would have been possible without the help of so many of my friends, family and supporters.

I want to thank my husband, Chris, for all the time and effort he has put into helping me proofread this book. I want to give thanks to my family in China: my father, Yuan Xiao Guo, my stepmother, Zhou Li, and my mother, Chen Shu Qin. They inspired my love of good food and cooking since I was a child. My kids, Oscar, Juliet, Sydney and Wendy, are my taste-testers and helped me refine the flavors of my recipes. Thanks to Josh Stokes, who shot the beautiful book cover for me.

Thanks to everyone on the Page Street Publishing team who helped me so much. Special thanks to Editorial Director Marissa Giambelluca and Creative Director Meg Baskis for their wonderful support and guidance.

Finally, I want to thank my social media supporters for following my journey of writing this book. It would not have been possible without your immense support and encouragement. Thank you for your ideas and opinions.

ABOUT THE AUTHOR

Vivian Aronson was born in Chengdu, China, and came to the United States in 2005. She learned to cook from her family, especially her grandmother and her aunt and uncle, who own and operate several restaurants in China. She started cooking on social media in 2018 and now posts on YouTube, Instagram and TikTok as @CookingBomb. She was selected for season ten of *Master Chef* and has been featured on the *Drew Barrymore Show*. In addition to cooking, Vivian has taught painting and designed her own clothing line. She currently lives with her husband and four children in Minneapolis, Minnesota.

INDEX